# The Management of Capital Projects

# The Management of Capital Projects

**M. F. Culpin**

**BSP PROFESSIONAL BOOKS**

OXFORD LONDON EDINBURGH

BOSTON MELBOURNE

First published 1989

British Library
Cataloguing in Publication Data
Culpin, M. F.
    Management of capital projects
    1. Financial management
    I. Title
    658.1.′5

ISBN 0-632-02599-9

BSP Professional Books
A division of Blackwell Scientific
    Publications Ltd
Editorial Offices:
Osney Mead, Oxford OX2 0EL
    (Orders: Tel. 0865 240201)
8 John Street, London WC1N 2ES
23 Ainslie Place, Edinburgh EH3 6AJ
3 Cambridge Center, Suite 208, Cambridge,
    MA 02142, USA
667 Lytton Avenue, Palo Alto, California
    94301, USA
107 Barry Street, Carlton, Victoria 3053,
    Australia

Set by Mathematical Composition Setters Ltd,
Salisbury, Wilts.

Printed and bound in Great Britain by
Mackays of Chatham PLC, Chatham, Kent

# Contents

Acknowledgements      vi

Introduction      vii

## Part I The Owner

| | | |
|---|---|---|
| 1 | Classification of Capital Projects | 3 |
| 2 | Synopsis of a Typical Project | 7 |
| 3 | Terminology of Capital Projects | 12 |
| 4 | Estimation of Capital Cost | 18 |
| 5 | Tendering Procedures | 33 |

## Part II Owner and Main Contractor

| | | |
|---|---|---|
| 6 | Types of Contract | 41 |
| 7 | Contract Documents | 48 |

## Part III Main Contractor

| | | |
|---|---|---|
| 8 | Contractor's Cash Flows | 55 |
| 9 | Competitive Bidding for Contracts | 65 |
| 10 | Scheduling the Project | 73 |
| 11 | Controlling the Project | 90 |

## Part IV Owner and Main Contractor

| | | |
|---|---|---|
| 12 | Completion and Hand-Over | 105 |

Bibliography      108

# Acknowledgements

The author wishes to thank Mr A Lester and Butterworths, and the Controller of Her Majesty's Stationery Office for permission to make use of copyright material for Chapter 11; Professor R McCaffer and Blackwell Scientific Publications for the basis of Chapter 9; and The Institution of Chemical Engineers for parts of Chapter 4. Present and former colleagues may recognise some of the examples and exercises. It is very difficult to check whether or not any of them are original work and I trust they will accept collectively my warmest thanks, wherever due.

M F Culpin
University of Stirling

# Dedication

To the memory of Frank Bradbury, with gratitude.

# Introduction

It is some years since the teaching of business and management (B & M) subjects was directed almost entirely at post-experience students. B & M education is now expanding rapidly into undergraduate studies where many students as yet have had little experience, except as consumers, of the real world of commerce, manufacture and services. Clearly it is important that time should be spent on setting the scene at the start of these studies. Otherwise the student may find some of the techniques and procedures used by managers difficult to appreciate. Much of this scene, certainly where it concerns manufacture and services, is closely related to the terminology and practice of the different branches of engineering, of which many B & M students may have little prior knowledge.

An aspect of this scene that has not yet been well served, from the point of view of the undergraduate B & M student, is project management. Much attention has been given in professional circles to techniques for managing projects, but as a subject for study at undergraduate level they have lagged behind the techniques for managing manufacture. There, very often, emphasis is on repetitive operations at carefully chosen and fixed locations where machinery is permanently installed. Labour, materials and services (water, electricity, etc.) are brought to the machines and much attention is paid to making ongoing quantities of product of specified quality. A project, on the other hand, requires these inputs to be provided at a previously selected site where they may not already be available. At the finish, the delivered materials will have been used up, not to be replaced. The services may continue in use after the project work is complete but the special machinery and work force required for the project must be deployed elsewhere. So there are some management problems with a project that are quite different from the problems of managing a factory or a public service.

The word 'project' is used here as an abbreviation of 'capital project'. There are various other kinds, such as R & D (research and development), maintenance, new product launch, computer software, and management information systems, a list, with the addition of construction, used by the Association of Project Managers (APM). Some excellent books have been written about all of these but we shall not be concerned with them here.

It seems to be characteristic of books on capital projects that they are written very much from the point of view of the principal branch of engineering involved: civil, chemical, mechanical, and so on. This segmentation presents a difficulty for the student of management with little technical knowledge, but it does help to show that quite diverse kinds of capital project have many elements in common that distinguish them, as mentioned above, from the manufacturing environment. The distinction may be expressed in terms of physical science by saying that a project is a *transient*, with a well-defined start and finish, compared with which a manufacturing operation is intended to continue in a *steady state*.

Many students are at a pre-experience stage of their career when studying management. For them, books are available that generalise important aspects of production management at a suitable level. But there is no analogous treatment of the management of projects. This book is intended to make good this deficiency with regard to one of the categories in the APM list: construction. This is interpreted broadly to include all the types of projects mentioned in Chapter 1. The designation 'capital project' will, however, be preferred here to construction as it is intended to encompass the installation of machinery as well as the provision of buildings and other civil engineering works.

The text is not excessively long because there is a limit to how far the detailed procedures of management can be properly generalised to include a wide range of circumstances. Also, it is mainly concerned with the management science of capital projects, omitting most of the matters of organisation and personnel management that constitute the management politics of the project. These are likely to vary greatly in substance and in terminology from one firm to another and deserve a quite separate treatment.

To maintain a generality of treatment, not too closely related to any one type of project, few detailed descriptions of real projects have been included. For practical illustrations of the general principles the student should consult the works mentioned in the bibliography, some of which are referred to in the text.

The student should also take advantage of any opportunity to visit work in progress. Formal application for such visits is normally made to the main Contractor's Personnel Manager, rather than directly to the Site Agent. The Agent will not wish to have work interrupted more than is absolutely necessary. There is also an element of danger to be considered on a construction site so that a visit must be planned properly.

In an attempt to come to terms with the great variety of capital projects, we begin with a broad classification and proceed with a main list of things to be done in the course of the project. This is followed by a chapter on terminology. Going on to deal with matters in more detail, the text is written partly from the point of view of the Owner and partly from the point of view of the main Contractor. This helps to show where responsibilities lie. It also reduces ambiguity in discussion of costs, where it is easy to leave in doubt the answer to the question: cost to whom?

There is one other matter that must be mentioned. In the text that follows, firms or persons will be represented from time to time by masculine pronouns. This is to ease the flow of the discussion. No disrespect is intended to women Owners, Contractors, Engineers, Quantity Surveyors or Accountants.

# Part I
# The Owner

# Chapter 1

# Classification of Capital Projects

Many of the subjects available to the student in higher education are unfamiliar, in the sense that they have not been studied at school. This includes most of the professional subjects. Engineering may be an exception, as almost everyone has seen some mechanical or electrical device working, although perhaps not in the context of a large-scale manufacturing operation. Some major capital projects, on the other hand, are plainly visible. The progress of civil engineering work can often be followed, for example, when a motorway is being built. Shopping centres, supermarkets and public buildings can sometimes be seen going up. Part of the work may indeed involve that traditional public spectacle, the 'hole in the road'. All this implies that a student may be more aware of the world of capital projects than he or she realises and almost certainly more so than of manufacturing industry. The internal problems of organisation and scheduling of either are not, of course, apparent to the casual observer, but the overall objective of the immediate construction work of a capital project is often fairly obvious.

The enormous diversity of capital projects, each one being, in some respects at least, unique, leads to difficulties in presenting the subject. The following very rough classification is intended to provide a framework within which some of the features common to most projects may be studied. It also provides an opportunity to introduce some of the dramatis personae of the project scene. This is important, as this book has, in effect, two major subdivisions: one is written from the point of view of the Owner; the other from the point of view of the main Contractor. Their names appear with the classification in Figure 1.

The person or firm who requires the project to be carried out will be referred to as the Owner. The word 'client' (one who employs a professional adviser) is often used but may be ambiguous here: the Owner may be the client of a number of profes-

sional advisers, but has a particular relationship with the main
Contractor who organises the construction work of the project.
Usually the Contractor is in the construction industry and is the
client of a number of specialised sub-contractors. Figure 1 forms a
base from which to describe some of the procedures and practices
that may differ only in detail from one broad category of project
to another. Amongst these are cost estimation, tendering, type of
contract, conditions of contract, scheduling, cost control, and
hand-over procedures, a list that is not however exhaustive.

Figure 1 shows that the categories of projects overlap. Under
'transport', installing a railway system would call for a great deal
of civil engineering work, although mechanical engineering
features largely in such a service when it is running. Similarly,
in the case of 'energy supply', designing and running the facility
are likely to involve chemical engineering whilst the construction
calls for major civil and mechanical inputs. 'Buildings' has been
included to indicate a project of fairly modest size, of no great
novelty and undertaken in circumstances unlikely to present major
difficulties. It is a category distinct from major projects such as
bridges, canals or dams, where there may be problems of access,
geological formation, or possibly politics, in addition to problems
arising from the novelty of design and construction methods.

Capital projects related to manufacturing can be classified
broadly into those creating a facility for converting raw materials

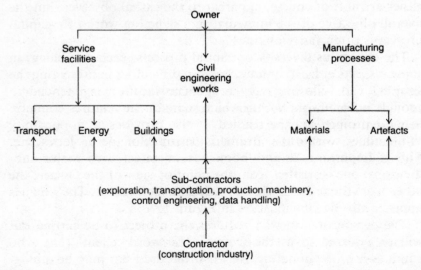

*Figure 1* A classification of capital projects

(e.g. metal ores, crude oil, green timber) into intermediate materials (e.g. sheet steel, polymer chips, paper) and those where the objective is to convert the intermediate material into a useful product (motor car components, plastic containers, books). The first largely embodies the principles of chemical engineering, with its unit processes and the handling, on a large scale and often under difficult physical conditions, of materials that may be hazardous. The second depends more on mechanical engineering and the shaping of materials by means of machine tools of various kinds, and by other methods.

At many points in this book the word 'construction' will be used, but it must not be assumed always to have the connotation of a project that is undertaken wholly within the construction industry. It may refer to part of a project, such as the foundations for a machine, which is otherwise mainly mechanical in nature.

Another way of classifying capital projects depends on the manner of involvement of the Owner. For example, a large firm may have the resources and expertise to be its own main Contractor for a project, appointing appropriate sub-contractors as necessary. Such a departmentalised project would be based on a project team composed of secondees from a number of the functions of the firm (e.g. production, R & D, engineering, marketing, accounts). The team would be led by a Project Manager specially appointed and usually, but not necessarily, from within the firm. So, for the duration of the project each member of the team will in fact be responsible to two bosses. It is therefore crucial that each departmental head from whom any of the team have been taken should be fully committed to the project. Ensuring commitment at this level is a problem for the board, not for the Project Manager who is likely to be fully occupied with keeping together a team whose members may, amongst other things, be required to work at least in part outside their usual range of expertise.

Sometimes, within the firm, the Project Manager is called the Project Engineer. This title must not be confused with the Engineer, the person or firm who is employed as a consultant by the Owner to instruct a main Contractor as work proceeds. The Engineer also has the important task of certifying the completion of the work by stages so that the Contractor may receive interim payments due in accordance with the contract.

In a design and build project the Contractor is closely involved in the design as well as the construction work. The Contractor may have experience and information related to a project that is not readily available to any independent firm of consulting engineers. The closeness of the relationship between Owner and Contractor ensures that the Owner gets exactly what is required from the Contractor: such closeness of working is recommended whenever possible.

At the other end of the spectrum from the early involvement of the Contractor is the turn-key project. In this type of project the Owner arrives at a well-defined and complete design in collaboration with the consultants. Only then is the work passed to the Contractor, who then assumes complete responsibility up to and including commissioning. Not only must the construction satisfy the Engineer, but, in the case of a manufacturing facility, the actual production of output of acceptable quality at an acceptable rate must be demonstrated. This is discussed in more detail in Chapter 12.

---

**Exercises**

1 Study local and national newspapers and journals for news of capital projects. Classify those that are found according to the criteria discussed in Chapter 1. Discuss, in general terms, their importance to the firms concerned, to the local community, and to the economy as a whole.

# Chapter 2

# Synopsis of a Typical Project

The history of a capital project is summarised in an idealised form in Figure 2. This shows a number of phases from initiation to hand-over. The pattern of procedures would almost certainly be less clear cut than this in real life where some phases might run more nearly concurrently with each other than is shown. Some might be omitted, others added, depending on the particular circumstances. Much of what is indicated in Figure 2, however, would occur at some time during the life of the project.

The term phase, rather than activity, has been used to avoid confusion with the activities carried out by the Contractor, and for which scheduling techniques are discussed in detail in Chapter 10. The phases of the project are indicated very broadly, and for each one the amount of work involved will differ from project to project, even within the categories discussed in Chapter 1.

The word 'initiation' shows that the project must have had a starting point at some time and place, but it may not be possible to define these precisely. It is more practical, if a statement is required, to take the view that the germ of the project probably emerged over time, from discussions amongst people in the various functions within the firm, corporation, government authority, or whoever is the Owner. Recognition of an opportunity, and the availability of resources, plus an accumulation of experience, leads to an idea that must then be subjected to increasingly rigorous scrutiny, as technical, financial and market information related to the project is collected.

A useful summary of the questions that must be asked and answered to the satisfaction of the board when seeking and evaluating the potential of new products can be found in Baines *et al*. (1969). This stage of a manufacturing project is discussed also in Twiss (1986).

Whilst technical feasibility is clearly of primary importance, in the case of a manufacturing facility, the question must also be

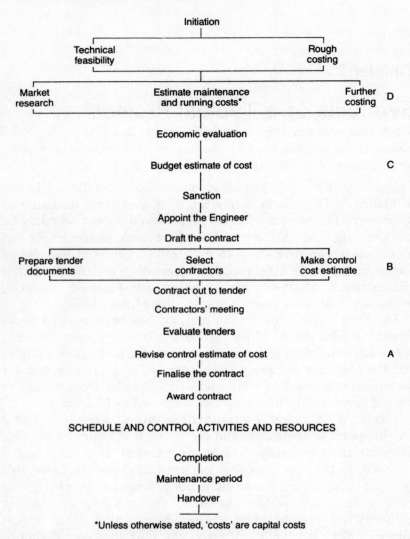

*Figure 2*   Outline history of a project

asked: is there enough evidence to suggest that the factory or process to make the product will work to the required specifications; and will the machinery be sufficiently reliable over the intended life-time of the plant? Or, in a civil engineering work, is it possible to achieve a safe design with the available materials; and is the proposed structure consistent with local geological conditions? These are matters for detailed study by engineers in the appropriate categories.

As work proceeds, data will become available from which initial costings may be made, sometimes known as ball park costings. Only a very rough estimate will be possible at this stage. Further refinements will be made in due course if the project is not abandoned for some reason. For satisfactory progress each phase must provide a basis for the next one. Otherwise, as definition of the project proceeds, and costs escalate, money may be wasted on work that will never be completed, or on doing the same work twice. If the project is to be abandoned,[1] a minimum of expense should have been incurred.

A project intended to provide a consumer product or service requires research into the potential market and an estimate of the costs of running and maintaining the facility, as well as the capital cost of the project. An exercise in capital budgeting will be required, of the kinds that are discussed in Bromwich (1976), for example. The results of this, together with an estimate of running cost, will lead to an estimate of the price to be charged for the product. Running costs are discussed by de la Mare (1982) and Clark & Lorenzoni (1985). For a manufacturing project in which production will build up over a number of years, the time value of money must be allowed for by discounting cash flows (see, for example, Allen (1985)).

The price must be considered to be satisfactory in relation to the results of market research, through surveys of various kinds, before the project is considered viable. In this area economics and sociology overlap. The reader will find a good indication of what is involved here in Crowson & Richards (1975) and in Baier (1985).

A project for a service such as a transport system might well be evaluated in the early stages in much the same way as described above. For a large civil engineering project, however, cost−benefit analysis (CBA) is likely to offer useful insights. Although the principles of CBA are applicable to a manufacturing project, there may be less tangible aspects to be considered (see Mishan (1972)). In addition, in the real world, political factors may be important.

Meanwhile, capital costings are further refined and consideration is given to possible sources of finance for the project. Definition of the successive stages of increased accuracy of capital cost estimating varies from author to author. They have been labelled in Figure 2 according to a scheme published by the Institution of Chemical Engineers (1982).

By combining these three aspects of the project (market research, running costs and capital costs) an overall economic evaluation is made. But a decision whether or not to proceed may well depend on factors other than the result of this evaluation. For example, the present status of the Owner in matters other than the project being currently considered; forecasts of future markets or demands; and the general economic climate, may all have influence. Assuming all is well, a further refinement of capital cost is made, sometimes referred to as the budget estimate. There are some more or less standardised procedures for estimating capital costs at this stage and some of them will be described in Chapter 4. Now the board of the Owner company makes the major decision of the project: to proceed, or not, with the necessary investment. Even at this stage it may not be an entirely clear-cut decision, particularly in the case of civil engineering work. A telling example is given by Thompson (1981:p110). Nevertheless, with sanction for the investment, what may be called the real work of the project may begin.

For projects other than in-house projects, there are now three main tasks to be done, all related to the main Contractor. The Owner has already done a great deal of work in defining the project. This must now be assembled into a number of tender documents to be sent to contractors who will be invited to bid for the contract. Not only is it crucial that the Owner should be absolutely clear what has to be done, but this must be made equally clear to a bidding contractor who, amongst other things, must also make an estimate of the cost so that a realistic price for the work can be calculated. The tender documents provide the information to enable these calculations to be worked out.

The Owner must now decide to which contractors the documents will be sent and must prepare yet another, even better, cost estimate (a project control estimate) for comparison with those that will be received from bidding contractors.

Following despatch of the documents, the Owner should call a meeting of contractors so that matters needing clarification may be discussed. The contractors who attend the meeting need not remain in the dark regarding any aspect of the project, and all of them will be able to bid on the basis of exactly the same information. They may assure themselves that they have been treated fairly by the Owner when they come to prepare their tenders.

In due course, tenders from some of the contractors will have to be evaluated. In the light of these, some of which may cause the Owner to revise the project control estimate of cost, the contract will be awarded.

From this point in the project it is convenient to begin to look at it from the Contractor's point of view, rather than the Owner's. The problems of scheduling and resource allocation are mainly the Contractor's, although the Owner will maintain an interest in how the work proceeds, especially if the contract is of the cost plus variety. The degree of Owner involvement depends on the type of project and the type of contract, but in all cases it is the function of the Engineer to keep the closest watch on what is happening.

Finally, the work is declared by the Engineer to be complete and the object of all the activity is handed over to the Owner. Again, the nature of these formalities will depend on the type of project, whether it is a factory for manufacture, a service facility, or a civil engineering work. Some examples of what is expected by the Owner are given in Chapter 12, but it is important to realise that they show only the main aspects of completion procedure and that these vary widely from one project to another.

## Exercises

These exercises will require some reading outside the list of titles in the bibliography.

1   In about 1000 words summarise the procedures involved in preparing an estimate of the running costs of a manufacturing facility.

2   Summarise the procedures for estimating the maintenance costs of a selected type of building or civil engineering structure.

3   Select a number of capital projects that have been completed in recent years, or about which discussion is proceeding in public, and comment on any information you can find about the technical feasibility of the project at the initiation stage.

4   What kinds of market research do you think was, or should be, done in the early stages of the projects you selected for Exercise 3?

# Chapter 3

# Terminology of Capital Projects

To assist the reader who is not familiar with the language of capital projects, this chapter takes the form of a glossary, but with more extensive definitions than are usually found in a glossary. There are four sets of definitions related respectively to general matters, accountancy, civil engineering projects, and process plant projects. Although only two of the project types shown in Figure 1 are mentioned here, in two of the sets most of the definitions are of general applicability.

This chapter may be regarded as an extended check list of terms in frequent use in connection with capital projects. In an exercise as large and complicated as a capital project, it is important to make use of check lists to ensure that nothing is forgotten at any stage. Figure 2 is a check list, but of such major items that it is unlikely that any of them will be forgotten in a real-life situation. Some other major check lists are given in Chapters 5 and 7 in relation to tender documents and contract documents. The latter include one of the most important check lists, the standard conditions of contract, where it is particularly important that the terms used are unambiguous.

Advantage should always be taken of the experience embodied in check lists and standard procedures, to save time and avoid repeating mistakes. The following glossary is in effect a skeleton list of matters that have to be considered in the course of the project, complementing the list in Figure 2.

## 1 General

*Owner* The person, firm or authority who requires the project to be carried out, and who will benefit from its completion. The Owner is a client of the main contractor and may well carry on his or her normal business with existing facilities whilst the project is in hand.

*Sanction*   Formal approval by the Owner (i.e. the board of the firm) of investment in the project. After this, the real work begins.

*Definition*   A project is commonly defined under three headings: scope, cost and time. The last two will be discussed in the following chapters, whereas the scope is very specific to a particular project (see 3 and 4 below).

*Main Contractor*   The firm to whom the main contract is awarded and who is responsible for all the work being done, including work done by sub-contractors. The main Contractor appoints the sub-contractors, pays them, and through the Engineer takes into account any special wishes of the Owner.

*The Engineer*   The person, or firm, employed by the Owner to instruct the main Contractor and to certify the satisfactory completion of work. Although employed by the Owner, the Engineer is expected to be impartial between the Owner and the Contractor. After a part of the work is completed and certified as satisfactory by the Engineer, the Owner makes interim payments to the Contractor, in accordance with the terms of the contract. The Engineer may, in addition to these functions, be acting in a consulting capacity to the Owner.

*The Architect*   In building projects, as distinct from civil engineering, the function of the Engineer is usually carried out by the Architect. The Architect may also play a part in other projects, particularly regarding environmental and aesthetic questions.

*Quantity Surveyor*   A cost consultant to the Owner in matters of civil engineering and building in the early stages of the project. The Quantity Surveyor (QS) prepares bills of quantities, and contributes to the budget estimate by applying realistic unit rates (see Chapter 4). The QS assists in the evaluation of tenders (see Chapter 5).

*Sub-contractor*   A person or firm specialising in particular aspects of the work to be done. The Sub-contractor is responsible directly to, and is paid by, the main Contractor.

*Estimate*   An estimate of cost. The Contractor's estimate of cost to himself includes any payments to be made to sub-contractors. The cost to the Owner (the price asked) will be the Contractor's estimate, plus a mark-up, to cover the Contractor's overheads and profit. The Owner's estimates of cost to himself should allow for this.

*Tender*   An application by a main Contractor to the Owner for award of the contract. The Owner invites a main Contractor to tender for the contract, or puts a contract out to tender.

*Let/award*   The contract is let, or awarded, by the Owner to the main Contractor, much as a house may be let from a proprietor to a tenant.

*Value*   The value to the Contractor of the work done so far is what he will be paid for it (i.e. the interim part of the price asked from the Owner). On completion of the project, the total value in the case of a lump sum contract is the price, based on estimates of cost plus the mark-up, originally asked by the Contractor, provided there have been no complications. (See Chapter 6.)

*Mark-up*   This is the amount added by the Contractor to the estimate of cost in a lump sum contract in arriving at the tender price to the Owner. It must cover overheads and profit. Much depends on the accuracy of an estimate and the choice of mark-up. (See Chapter 9.)

*Contribution*   The actual mark-up achieved by the Contractor from a lump sum contract (i.e. the price eventually paid by the Owner, less the total costs actually incurred by the Contractor). It is what contributes to overheads and profit in the final accounts and can be more or less than the original mark-up. In exceptional circumstances the contribution can be negative.

*Certification*   Formal acknowledgement by the Engineer that the work done is satisfactory and that the Contractor is entitled to an interim, or final, payment by the Owner. Payment is often on a monthly basis with time lags and retentions as provided by the contract. (See Chapter 8.)

## 2 Accountancy

The Owner, the main Contractor, and the sub-contractors are all concerned with accountancy if their businesses are to be controlled properly. In practice it is convenient to consider two kinds of accountancy, of equal importance, but rather different in nature. A good account of these in relation to the construction industry is given in Woodward (1975).

*External accounting*  This is the kind of accounting practised by professional accountants. It is necessary for a number of practical as well as legal reasons. The state of the finances of the Owner firm is required to be known with accuracy at least once a year. The Owner needs to know how the firm is faring. The Owner may have shareholders expecting a dividend. And the Inland Revenue and Customs & Excise must be paid what is due to them, according to the law. Thus, by a slow and expensive procedure, information is assembled and processed to ensure that the correct sums are paid, no more and no less. For the day-to-day control of a project, however, all this is unsatisfactory. Great accuracy is not needed for project control, and if appropriate controlling action is to be taken, questions must be asked and answered quickly, in days rather than months. (See Chapter 11.)

*Internal accounting*  To measure progress within the project, and check against wastage of materials, labour, or plant time, fast and cheap methods are required that can be carried out by technical staff. Methods straightforward enough for technical staff to use have the additional advantage that their experience enables them to appraise the status of the project more realistically than might reasonably be expected of a professional accountant. It is often said that the success of a business depends more on effective "coarse" accountancy than on the professional kind. All the calculations in the later chapters involving finance are of the coarse variety.

## 3 Civil Engineering

The following definitions have been compiled for easy reference from a number of sources that are not always quite consistent with each other. When using the bibliography the reader is advised to watch for differences from one text to another. It is not uncommon for more than one word to be used for the same thing even within one text.

*Scope*   In the contract: specifications of the objectives of the project; the type of contract (see Chapter 6); the starting date; the definition of completion. In the site data: location, geographical and geological features of the site, access facilities.

*Site*   The area within which all the work of the project is to be carried out. In populated areas the site should be clearly marked out, and persons not directly involved in the project warned of possible dangers. The main Contractor may disclaim responsibility for accidents to persons disregarding a warning.

*Project Manager*   A senior member of the main Contractor's staff who has authority to act on behalf of the main Contractor in all matters related to the contract. The Project Manager does not usually work on the site on a day-to-day basis.

*Site Agent*   A less senior member of the main Contractor's staff who is located on site in normal working hours for the duration of the project to supervise the work. The Site Agent liaises with, and receives instructions from, the Engineer.

*Plant*   All machinery used for construction purposes, including excavators, drilling machines, cranes, bulldozers, earth-movers, pile drivers, concrete mixers, elevators, etc.

*Materials*   All building materials, such as brick, stone, facing materials; components of concrete (aggregate, sand, cement, additives); scaffolding for false work; timber for form work; reinforcement materials, etc.

## 4   Process Plant

With some modifications and additions the definitions given above in relation to civil engineering apply also to process plant projects.

*Scope*   For a process plant project the scope includes data and specifications concerning the plant to be installed, such as type, size, preferred suppliers of machinery; rates of production, properties of the product; and documentation of site plans, plant lay-out, process flow sheets, maintenance instructions, etc.

*Site*   The location where the plant will be built.

*Plant* This is now as defined in the scope of the project, and is part of the works.

*Works* All the Contractor's plant, equipment and services for the time being on site, plus the plant that is being constructed for the Owner, at whatever stage it may have reached.

*Materials* Includes everything required to construct or modify the building to house the plant, and the components to be assembled into the plant itself.

### Exercises

1   Some of the subjects of the definitions in this chapter are of consequence throughout the project, whilst for others the significance varies from one phase to another. Draw a set of boxes alongside a copy of Figure 2 and allocate each subject to an appropriate box or boxes. For example, the word 'tender' should appear in several boxes near the centre of the diagram, whereas 'let/award' should appear in only one or two or them.

2   Write a short essay on the relationships within the context of a capital project amongst the main Contractor, the Quantity Surveyor, and the consulting Engineer.

# Chapter 4

# Estimation of Capital Cost

To assess the financial implications of the project, the Owner and Contractor both need to know as accurately as possible how much they will have to spend on it. Because the Contractor will expect to earn a contribution to overheads and profit, the Owner will spend more than the Contractor.

In the early stages following initiation, the design work has only just started, but it will then proceed in greater detail, perhaps right up to the time of completion in the case of minor features. In these early stages estimates of cost are likely to prove to have been very inaccurate, but they are necessary if the project is to start at all. It has been seen already (Chapter 2) that improved estimates of cost are still being made after the work has actually been sanctioned. The way in which design work and cost estimation are related over time is shown in Figure 3a. Figure 3b shows corresponding curves concerning cost control, to which reference is made in Chapter 11. Completion of the design, and the most accurate estimate of cost, may not be reached until after the contract has been awarded.

Accurate estimation of the cost of a capital project is a highly complex operation, requiring knowledge of the nature of the project, familiarity with standard procedures for making the estimate, and the skill derived from experience to ensure that nothing has been omitted. Usually the Owner does not have the full expertise to arrive at the budget estimate and depends very much on the consulting Engineer and Quantity Surveyor at this stage. Increasingly accurate costings should be available to the Owner, certainly at the time when the contractors' tenders are received (see Chapter 9). Eventually the Contractor will be able to make the most accurate estimates, provided the Owner's specifications are complete, because he has inside information about the work to be done, based on experience.

Provision is made for inaccuracy in the early stages by adding a contingency allowance as a percentage of the estimate. The

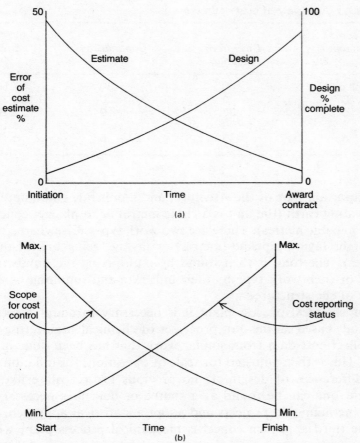

*Figure 3*   (a) Design and accuracy of estimate against time; (b) cost control and reporting against time

magnitude of the errors expected, and the allowances made for them, are shown in Table 1, which also gives a rough time scale. It is clear that accuracy better than the budget estimate C takes a considerable time. The cost of making the budget estimate for a civil engineering project, including the Quantity Surveyor's fees, is generally taken to be about 0.25% of the capital cost, or £25 000 for a £10 million project.

There are three main ways of approaching the problem of cost estimation. The first applies to civil engineering or building work. Each main part of the structure is divided into work types so that each part may be seen as consisting of measurable numbers of identifiable units of work. A unit rate for each unit of work is calculated, based on current prices. For example, foundations are

TABLE 1 Accuracy of cost estimate

| Type of estimate (Figure 2) | Days from initiation | Contingency % | Error % |
|---|---|---|---|
| 'Ball park' | 0 | + 30 | ± 50 |
| D | 2 | + 20 | ± 30 |
| C | 30 | + 10 | ± 20 |
| B | 200 | + 5 | ± 10 |
| A | 400 | + 5 | ± 5 |

an important part of the structure, and a unit rate could apply to excavating earth (the unit is a cubic metre) or to placing concrete (also in cubic metres). These are two work types. Elsewhere, items might be laying pipeline (metres) or laying facing brick (square metres). The total is then found by multiplying the numbers of units of each work type by their unit rate and summing over all parts of the structure.

For chemical process plant it is necessary to adopt a second method, based on the unit processes of chemical engineering and to collect cost data from similar work that has been done in the past. This is then adjusted for scale of operation, for inflation and for differences of design. If no previous project quite like the present one can be found as a source of data it is necessary to examine many old projects and adopt a statistical approach.

The third approach concerns mechanical process plant where the diversity of operations is so great that the concept of the unit process is not applicable. Estimation begins with machinery to be bought from a specialist supplier who can quote catalogue prices. Allowance is then made for associated civil engineering work, power supplies, ventilation, etc.

## Civil Engineering Work and Buildings

The problem of sub-division of a project has been discussed in the section above. As mentioned in Chapter 2, in some of the projects that are readily visible to the general public it is not difficult to see how the work may be separated into parts. For example, the foundations, walls, drainage system and roof are identifiable parts, for each of which various work types are needed, that can be expressed in numbers of appropriate units. The necessary skills are provided by the Quantity Surveyor.

   To estimate the total cost it is necessary to find these numbers of units from the drawings and specifications of the project and to compile a bill of quantities (BOQ) of work types for each part. The cost of each part may be found by adding up for each part the quantity of work type multiplied by the unit rate. There may be differences between the unit rates used by the Quantity Surveyor for the budget estimate and those used by the Contractor for tendering purposes. Two simple examples illustrate the procedure.

   The first example is a brick wall of a standard type, built on a standard foundation. Usually the unit rates for the foundation and the wall would already be known so that only the last lines of the following calculation would be done. However, calculation of some unit rates is shown here as part of the estimating procedure. It is quite clear that a computing facility would be valuable in handling a large number of items and suitable software packages are available.

### Example 1
Brick wall, double cavity 60 m × 2.5 m
(120 bricks/m$^2$) on a standard concrete foundation 0.5 m × 0.8 m

Calculation of unit rates for wall with foundation

Work type: foundation 0.5 × 0.8 m          The unit is 1 m.

|  |  | cost/h | h/unit | cost/unit |
|---|---|---|---|---|
| LABOUR | excavate | 6.20 | 0.08 | 0.50 |
|  | place concrete | 5.78 | 0.14 | 0.81 |
|  |  | cost/m$^3$ | m$^3$/unit | cost/unit |
| MATERIALS | concrete | 21.00 | 0.40 | 8.40 |
|  |  | cost/h | h/unit | cost/unit |
| PLANT | excavator | 24.75 | 0.08 | 1.98 |

COST/UNIT OF FOUNDATION = £11.69

Work type: wall double cavity          The unit is 1m$^2$

|  |  | cost/h | h/unit | cost/unit |
|---|---|---|---|---|
| LABOUR | unloading | 2.50 | 0.02 | 0.05 |
|  | bricklayer | 4.25 | 1.8 | 7.65 |
|  |  | costs | quan/unit | cost/unit |
| MATERIALS | mortar | £25/m$^3$ | 0.045m$^3$ | 1.13 |
|  | bricks | £100/1000 | 120 NR | 12.00 |

COST/UNIT OF WALL = £20.83

### BOQ for Example 1

Wall, double cavity $\quad\quad 60 \times 2.5 = 150 \text{ m}^2$

Foundation 0.5 m × 0.8 m $\quad\quad\quad\quad 60$ m

UNIT RATES: 1 m$^2$ wall, double cavity $\quad\quad$ £20.83

1 m foundation 0.5 m × 0.8 m $\quad$ £11.69

COST OF EXAMPLE 1 $\quad = 150 \times £20.83 + 60 \times £11.69 = £3826$

## Example 2

A set of twelve reinforced concrete
stanchions, 0.5 m × 0.5 m, each 3.2 m high

Calculation of unit rate for stanchion. The unit is 1 m of
stanchion.

Work type: reinforcement

|  |  | Cost/unit of input | Required/unit of work type | Cost/unit of work type |
|---|---|---|---|---|
| LABOUR | constructor | £4.5/h | 0.6 h | £2.70 |
|  | labourer | £2.7/h | 0.6 h | £1.62 |
| MATERIAL | steel bar | £1.2/m | 16 m | £19.20 |
|  | tie wire | £0.8/kg | 1.3 kg | £1.04 |

Work type: shuttering

|  |  |  |  |  |
|---|---|---|---|---|
| LABOUR | carpenter | £3.5/h | 2 h | £7.00 |
|  | labourer | £2.5/h | 2 h | £5.00 |
| MATERIAL | sheet | £1.9/m$^2$ | 2.3 m$^2$ | £4.37 |
|  | battens | £0.35/m | 7 m | £2.45 |

Work type: concrete

|  |  |  |  |  |
|---|---|---|---|---|
|  | transport | £3.1/m$^3$ | 0.25 m$^3$ | £0.78 |
|  | placing | £4.2/m$^3$ | 0.25 m$^3$ | £1.05 |
|  | mix | £15/m$^3$ | 0.25 m$^3$ | £3.75 |

Work type: strike

|  |  |  |  |  |
|---|---|---|---|---|
|  | labour | £2.8/h | 0.4 h | £1.12 |

COST UNIT OF STANCHION = £50.08

### BOQ for Example 2

12 × 3.2 m of standard 0.5 m × 0.5 m stanchion

COST OF EXAMPLE 2 = 12 × 3.2 × £50.08 = £19 231

(where £50.08 is the unit cost as calculated above)

It is easy to imagine the extent and complexity of the calculations of cost estimates for any substantial project. Standardisation of the way in which the work may be divided into types or categories, and the way in which bills of quantities are set out, make for more reliable estimating. In some parts of the project, however, it may be impossible to draw up a bill of quantities of work types in advance of the work being done. For example, there may be geological reasons why the extent of an excavation, and the volume of concrete needed to fill it, cannot be foreseen accurately. The price to be paid for these parts is then calculated on the basis of unit rates and admeasurement of the work actually done. Standard procedures for admeasurement are the subject of a document prepared by the Institution of Civil Engineers (ICE) known as CESMM (1985). For the budget estimate, the unit rates used may be only the best available to the Quantity Surveyor. The unit rates used by the Contractor prior to tendering will be more realistic, but neither party will know what unit rates have been used by the other at that stage. Eventually, agreed unit rates may be incorporated in the contract. There is further reference to these matters in Chapter 7 which deals with conditions of contract.

## Chemical Process Plant

Much of the equipment of the chemical industry consists of the means of carrying out unit processes. Important examples are reaction vessels, distillation columns, filter presses and pumps. A particular chemical product is made by an array of unit processes, each with its supporting structure, pipework, and electrical and control equipment. These ancillary items will be referred to as peripherals. As the chemical industry developed it was found that the cost of a plant that differed only in size from an existing plant could be represented sufficiently well in feasibility studies by a simple exponential formula (see IChemE 1982:p13 and Hackney 1965:p31).

$$[\text{Cost for capacity } C_2] = [\text{cost for capacity } C_1] \times [C_2/C_1]^{2/3}$$

This formula is intended to take account at once of the total cost of all the unit processes required to make the product, each with its own peripheral equipment. Not surprisingly it takes an over-simplified view of chemical plant and its components and has been overtaken by a progression of more sophisticated methods. A partial justification for the 2/3 exponent can be found in de la Mare (1982).

With further development, and more manufacturers of unit process equipment, it became possible for the maker to quote a price for a unit of a certain size. This price does not include peripherals, however. To allow for these Lang (1948) found that a price that included buildings and services could be found by using one of a number of 'Lang factors'.

The delivered cost was to be multiplied by a factor that depends on the general nature of the materials handled within the process:

|  | Factor |
| --- | --- |
| Solids | 3.1 |
| Solids and liquids | 3.6 |
| Liquids | 4.7 |

The delivered cost was taken as the sum of the purchase price (usually Free On Board (FOB) which includes handling and loading at the makers), freightage and insurance.

These rather crude factors were based on analysis of the data available at the time, and without the benefit of computing facilities for handling the information. Not surprisingly, they also were found to be inadequate and further improvements were needed. With this aim, features were sought that different chemical plants have in common. Data from these features in existing plant could then be transferred to proposals for a new plant. Attempts were made to represent peripherals by factors that remain roughly constant from one plant to another of a particular type. Miller factors (Miller 1965) are the first example.

Miller assumed that the capital cost of the part of the plant where most of the production costs arise, the so-called battery limits area, is known from a maker's quotation. Miller then found that sums in proportion to this bought cost must be added to allow for storage and handling, for utilities (such as sanitation, medical centre, canteen), and for services (such as water, electricity, access roads). Representing these various costs by initials, the total cost could be written as

$$TC = BL \times [1 + S\&H + U + S]$$

The Miller factors appear in the formula as terms, each in turn multiplying the battery limits cost BL. Exercises at the end of the chapter show how the factors work in practice.

Many other ways have been tried to find a quick method of

getting a guesstimate of capital costs at an early stage of a feasibility study. Hackney (1965:p31) quotes a case where an allowance of $1 million per foot of process flow chart gave not unreasonable results. More scientific is the method of the Guthrie modules (Guthrie 1969). Again, it is a question of assembling as much historical data as possible to identify factors that can be applied to a proposed new project.

The peripherals of a chemical processing plant are put under several headings.

| | |
|---|---|
| Solids handling | Direct |
| Site development | cost |
| Industrial buildings | factors |
| Off-site facilities | |
| | |
| Geological exploration | Indirect |
| Insurance | cost |
| | factors |

Thus, a formula for installed cost emerges

Installed cost = [bought cost of unit processes]
   × [1 + sum of direct factors]
   × [1 + sum of indirect factors]

summed over all unit processes.

More recently, accumulation of data, and computing facilities for handling it, enable a more direct approach to be made. Cost factors for the peripherals of a number of different types of unit process may, for example, come under the following headings.

| | Factors for a heat exchanger (carbon steel) |
|---|---|
| Piping | 0.35 |
| Instrument-ation | 0.15 |
| Civil work | 0.10 |
| Buildings | 0.05 |
| Insulation | 0.15 |
| Electric light | 0.05 |
| Painting | 0.05 |
| | 0.90 |

As different materials may be used for the unit process, a further factor may be required (IChemE 1982:p18). Factors in the list above are related to a unit made of carbon steel. The peripherals are expected to be affected by the type of unit, but not by the price of the unit. Before the above factors could be applied to the price of a bronze unit, say, which is more expensive than a carbon steel one, they must be scaled down. A factor of 0.65 is suggested. The following example shows the procedure.

### Estimated cost of a heat exchanger

| CARBON STEEL | bought cost | = £17 500 |
| | sum of factors above | = 0.90 |
| | installed cost | = 17 500 × [1 + 0.9] |
| | | = £33 250 |

| BRONZE | material factor | = 0.65 |
| | bought cost | = £26 900 |
| | adjusted bought cost | = 26 900 × 0.65 |
| | | = £17 500 |
| | installed cost | = 26 900 + 17 500 × 0.9 |
| | | = £42 630 |

| or, simply, | installed cost | = £26 900 × [1 + 0.9 × 0.65] |
| | | = £42 630 |

It must be emphasised that the above short cuts to an estimate of capital cost are entirely dependent on historical data from previous projects, and on the assumption that the data are applicable, via the various factors, to the present project. Much skill, based on experience, is needed for accurate estimating. All authors agree that human judgement in relation to the data is equally as important as the data themselves, or the computer, in doing the calculations.

## Mechanical Process Plant

A substantial part of the cost of setting up a factory containing machinery arises from building and civil engineering work. For these, estimating procedures as outlined above may be used. To these must be added the cost of the items of machinery themselves, and the cost of installation, and of all the peripheral equipment for services and control purposes. Further consideration of the costings would involve the detail of engineering matters that are beyond the scope of the present discussion, which is intended to give a general view of some aspects of project management. Therefore the question of mechanical process plant will not be taken any further.

## Exercises

1 A particular type of chemical plant has been found to vary in capital cost, excluding peripherals, according to the 0.62 power of the capacity. A plant with a capacity of 2300 tonnes per year is known to have cost £1.75 million. What is the anticipated cost of similar plants that will make (a) 3200 tonnes and (b) 7000 tonnes per year? Comment on the accuracy of the estimate for the 7000 tonnes plant.

2 The type of plant referred to in Exercise 1 involves the handling of solids and liquids so that to take peripherals into account in estimating costs a Lang factor of 3.6 is used. Using this information, what would now be the installed cost of plants of capacity (a) 3200 tonnes and (b) 7000 tonnes per year?

3 Suppose the existing plant costs in Exercise 1 are for the battery limits of the plant as defined by Miller. For this type of plant the Miller factors for storage and handling, utilities, and services are 0.15, 0.23 and 0.28 respectively. What installed costs do these factors give for the plants of (a) 3200 tonnes and (b) 7000 tonnes per year?

4 A new chemical process plant is to be built on a green-field site. An estimate of cost of all equipment in the battery limits area (BL) is £2.5 million. Storage and handling will be expensive, as raw materials and product are almost entirely liquid phase, so that a factor of 65% is appropriate. There is nothing exceptional about the utilities required (factor 25%) and the services are of standard kinds (factor 15%). Find a factored estimate for the complete plant, allowing 15% for contingencies.

5 A chemical plant for making pigments has proved more efficient than expected so that the final filter press has become a bottle neck. It is proposed to add a similar filter press in parallel, together with a pump to feed it. When the existing press and its pump were bought two years ago

they cost £5700 and £1500 respectively, FOB. Transport cost for the two items together was £520.

Both items are to be made of stainless steel. Find the factored estimate of the installed cost of the two new items, allowing 25% for inflation and 5% for contingencies, given the following peripheral factors, based on carbon steel equipment, and the material factors.

|  |  | Pump | Filter |
|---|---|---|---|
| Peripherals | Piping | 0.30 | 0.25 |
|  | Instrumentation | 0.10 | 0.10 |
|  | Civil | 0.05 | 0.05 |
|  | Effluent | — | 0.35 |
|  | Power supply | 0.02 | 0.02 |
|  |  |  |  |
| Material factors | Carbon steel | 1.0 | 1.0 |
|  | Stainless steel | 0.7 | 0.5 |
|  | Case hardened steel | 0.9 | — |
|  | Bronze | 0.65 | — |

6  Calculate a unit rate, i.e. cost/unit of work type, for 200 mm thick reinforced concrete floor, given the following data. The unit is $1 \text{ m}^2$ for this work type.

The cost of reinforcement per unit is made up of labour and materials, for which the rates and requirements per unit are:

| LABOUR | Constructor | £6.2/h | 0.4 h |
|---|---|---|---|
|  | Labourer | £3.6/h | 0.4 h |
| MATERIALS | Steel bar | £1.3/m | 12 m |
|  | Tie wire | £1.4/kg | 1.5 kg |

The concrete may be obtained as a ready-mix, at £21/m³, and requiring $0.2 \text{ m}^3$ per unit. The mix would be delivered to the site of the floor.

Alternatively, materials may be bought, and a mixer and a tipper truck hired. Thus:

| MATERIALS | Aggregate | £2.7/m³ | 0.10 m³ |
|---|---|---|---|
|  | Sand | £3.4/m³ | 0.06 m³ |
|  | Cement | £14.7/m³ | 0.06 m³ |
| PLANT | Mixer | £10.5/h | 0.25 h |
|  | Tipper | £8.4/h | 0.10 h |
| LABOUR | Operator | £7.3/h | 0.07 h |
|  | Driver | £6.9/h | 0.03 h |

Once the mixed concrete is at the floor site it must be conveyed in barrows and placed. The costs here are labour costs.

| | | |
|---|---|---|
| Labourer | £3.6/h | 0.15 h |
| Placer | £5.8/h | 0.20 h |

Which source of concrete is the cheaper? Using that one, what is the unit rate for the floor?

7   A chemical process plant is to be extended with the addition of a storage tank, feed pump and a refining column. To estimate the cost of this work, including the peripherals, data are to be taken from Tables 2(a) and 2(b) on pages 30–1 and 32 (IChemE 1982).

The costing is best done by completing the table below, taking the appropriate factors as found on pages 30–1 and 32.

| Main plant item (MPI) | | Storage tank | Feed pump | Refining column |
|---|---|---|---|---|
| Material | | CS | SS 410 | SS 316 |
| Cost of MPI (£) | | 39 000 | 1800 | 32 600 |
| Factor for CS | | _____ | _____ | _____ |
| Adjusted cost of MPI | (1) | _____ | _____ | _____ |
| | | | Factors | |
| *Peripherals* | | | | |
| Erection of MPI | | _____ | _____ | _____ |
| Piping | | _____ | _____ | _____ |
| Instruments | | _____ | _____ | _____ |
| Electrical | | _____ | _____ | _____ |
| Civil | | _____ | _____ | _____ |
| Building | | _____ | _____ | _____ |
| Lagging | | _____ | _____ | _____ |
| Total factor | (2) | _____ | _____ | _____ |
| Peripherals cost | (1) × (2) | _____ | _____ | _____ |
| *Installed MPI cost* | | _____ | _____ | _____ |
| TOTAL COST | | | | _____ |

---

* Tables 2(a) and 2(b) are reproduced by kind permission of the Institution of Chemical Engineers. They originally appeared in *A new guide to capital costing* which is published by, and available from, the Institution.

| | Value of individual main plant item, revised to CS basis (see Table 2(b)) (vessels, furnaces, machines and drives materials handling equipment) |
|---|---|
| Main plant items Erection | Much of site erection included in purchase cost of equipment e.g. large tanks |
| | Average erection |
| | Equipment involving some site fabrication e.g. large pumps requiring lining up serpentine coolers |
| | Equipment involving much site fabrication or fitting e.g. large distillation columns, furnaces |
| | At discretion of estimator, interpolation may be made. |
| Piping ducting and chutes including erection | Ducting and chutes |
| | Small bore piping or service piping only |
| | Average bore piping and service piping (e.g. predominantly liquid piping) |
| | Large bore piping and service piping (e.g. predominently gas and vapour piping) or |
| | Average bore piping with complex system (e.g. much manifolding, recirculation etc.) |
| | Large bore piping complex system (e.g. much manifolding, recirculation, etc.) |
| | Multiply piping factors by 1.3 for special pipe materials or steam tracing |
| Instruments | Local instruments only |
| | 1 controller and instruments |
| | 2 controllers and instruments |
| | 3 or more controllers and instruments |
| Electrical | Lighting only |
| | Lighting and power for ancillary drives (e.g. conveyors, stirred vessels, air coolers, etc.) |
| | Lighting and power *excluding* transformers and switchgear (i.e. this equipment off site) for machine main drives (e.g. pumps, compressors, crushers, etc.) |
| | Lighting and power *including* transformers and switchgear for machine main drives (e.g. pumps, compressors, crushers, etc.) |
| Civil | Average civil work, incl. plant and structure foundations, floors and services |
| | Above average civil work, complicated machine blocks, special floor protection, elevator pits in floors, considerable services. |
| | Multiply civil factor by 1.3 to allow for piling plant and structure foundations |
| Structures and buildings | Negligible structural work and buildings |
| | Open air plant at ground level with some pipebridges and minor buildings |
| | Open air plant within a structure |
| | Plant in a simple covered building |
| | Plant in an elaborate building or on a major structure within a building |
| Lagging | Lagging for service pipes only |
| | Average amount of hot lagging on pipes and vessels |
| | Above average amount of hot lagging on pipes and vessels |
| | Cold lagging on pipes and vessels |

| ef. | Over £150,000 | 50,000 150,000 | 20,000 50,000 | 10,000 20,000 | 3,000 10,000 | 1,500 3,000 | Under 1,500 |
|---|---|---|---|---|---|---|---|
| | 1.00 | 1.00 | 1.00 | 1.00 | 1.00 | 1.00 | 1.00 |
| 1 | .01 | .02 | .03 | .05 | .06 | .07 | .20 |
| 2 | .04 | .06 | .08 | .09 | .10 | .12 | .30 |
| 3 | .06 | .08 | .10 | .12 | .14 | .16 | .38 |
| 4 | .24 | .30 | .36 | .45 | .54 | .62 | .90 |
| 5 | .02 | .04 | .08 | .14 | .22 | .34 | .46 |
| 6 | .05 | .10 | .20 | .34 | .55 | .83 | 1.12 |
| 7 | .13 | .21 | .32 | .53 | .78 | 1.12 | 1.41 |
| 8 | .16 | .26 | .39 | .62 | .89 | 1.26 | 1.55 |
| 9 | .20 | .33 | .49 | .77 | 1.1 | 1.57 | 1.94 |
| 10 | | | | | | | |
| 11 | .02 | .03 | .05 | .10 | .19 | .34 | .60 |
| 12 | .07 | .10 | .18 | .27 | .39 | .52 | .80 |
| 13 | .10 | .16 | .26 | .36 | .48 | .63 | .91 |
| 14 | .15 | .26 | .35 | .48 | .62 | .77 | 1.10 |
| 15 | .02 | .02 | .03 | .05 | .08 | .10 | .15 |
| 16 | .08 | .11 | .16 | .21 | .27 | .33 | .48 |
| 17 | .10 | .14 | .20 | .26 | .34 | .41 | .50 |
| 18 | .15 | .20 | .27 | .37 | .48 | .59 | .80 |
| 19 | .06 | .08 | .11 | .14 | .18 | .22 | .28 |
| 20 | .12 | .17 | .25 | .32 | .40 | .48 | .68 |
| 21 | | | | | | | |
| 22 | .01 | .02 | .02 | .03 | .04 | .05 | .06 |
| 23 | .05 | .06 | .08 | .11 | .14 | .17 | .21 |
| 24 | .11 | .19 | .25 | .33 | .40 | .47 | .59 |
| 25 | .15 | .23 | .31 | .39 | .46 | .55 | .68 |
| 26 | .25 | .39 | .50 | .61 | .72 | .85 | 1.10 |
| 27 | .01 | .02 | .03 | .05 | .08 | .12 | .18 |
| 28 | .02 | .03 | .06 | .11 | .17 | .25 | .30 |
| 29 | .03 | .05 | .08 | .14 | .21 | .28 | .35 |
| 30 | .05 | .08 | .12 | .20 | .25 | .33 | .45 |

TABLE 2(b)   Typical multiplying factors for converting alloy and other fabricating costs to a carbon steel equivalent cost

| Material | | Pumps etc. | Other equipment |
|---|---|---|---|
| All carbon steel | | 1.0 | 1.0 |
| Stainless steel type | 410 | 0.7 | 0.5 |
| | 304 | 0.55 | 0.4 |
| | 316 | 0.5 | 0.35 |
| | 310 | 0.5 | 0.3 |
| Rubber lined steel | | 0.7 | 0.8 |
| Bronze | | 0.65 | |
| Monel | | 0.3 | |
| | | *Heat exchangers* | |
| Carbon steel shell and tubes | | 1.0 | |
| | Al tubes | 0.8 | |
| | Monel tubes | 0.48 | |
| | 304 stainless steel tubes | 0.6 | |
| 304 stainless steel shell and tubes | | 0.35 | |

# Chapter 5

# Tendering Procedures

Parts of Chapter 4 may be considered as written from either the Owner's or the Contractor's point of view. This chapter is very much concerned with actions by the Owner. A project for which the Owner does not have the expertise or resources requires the services of a main Contractor. Following sanction by the board, when the design and costing so far have met with approval, several things must be done (see Figure 2) with a view to seeking a main Contractor. Documents must be prepared and the contract put out to tender. This is done by invitation, or sometimes by an advertisement in the press to which anyone may reply. The latter procedure is known as open tendering.

More commonly, the Owner selects a small number of contractors, say, four, by the criteria given below. If a large number are invited, and all bid, then a large number will be unsuccessful. A major part of tendering is estimation of cost by the Contractor, and estimation has to be paid for, whether or not the contract is won. Thus, with large numbers of bids, prices to the Owner would be generally raised, so that when a contract is won, the estimating costs of both successful and unsuccessful bids are covered. So it is to the advantage of the Owner not to invite too many tenders.

The value of check lists has been emphasised already. This chapter is based on a number of these lists, where some of the items refer to specific actions and some are reminders of what constitutes good practice. To proceed, the Owner should work to a basic list of five actions.

1 Prepare the tender documents.
2 Select contractors for invitation to bid.
3 Hold a pre-tender meeting of these contractors.
4 Await and evaluate bids.
5 Award the contract.

## Tender Documents

There are several tender documents, in the preparation of which it would be prudent for the Owner to observe some basic rules, which have some general validity.

(a)   Ensure that all text is simple and unambiguous.

(b)   Check that drawings carry all necessary information and that where commonly agreed engineering standards and conditions of contract are referred to for brevity—e.g. from the BSI and the professional engineering institutions (see Chapter 7)—clear references are given.

(c)   Check all the tender documents for internal consistency. However much the Contractor wishes to win the contract, it should not be necessary to spend time on detective work to decide which of possible alternative statements is correct.

(d)   Specify a programme of key dates in the execution of the project and define completion so that the Contractor will be in no doubt how and when responsibilities will end if the contract is won.

There follows a list of likely tender documents, together with brief comments on each one.

### Letter of invitation

This is little more than a courtesy document, carrying an address, a date, and the invitation to tender for the contract.

### Conditions of tender

Conditions of tender are not to be confused with the conditions of contract. The intention here is to assure the potential bidder that his response to the invitation will be given fair treatment. For example, that the bid will receive full consideration and not be lightly passed over. Amongst other things there will be the date of a pre-tender meeting between the Owner, Consultants and Contractors, and a final date set for receiving bids.

### General conditions of contract

These are preferably in a standard form, as prepared by one or a group of the professional institutions, to reduce the chances of something important being omitted. The conditions are discussed in Chapter 7.

### Special conditions of contract

There may be features and circumstances peculiar to the project that are not covered by the general conditions. There is further discussion in Chapter 7.

### Plans, drawings and diagrams

These summarise the Owner's requirements into working documents, i.e. papers that can be used quickly and easily on a day-to-day basis. These are backed up by the Specifications.

### Specifications

This part of the documentation must contain everything the Contractor needs to know about dimensions, materials, procedures of construction, and standards of workmanship to enable correct judgement of whether or not he can complete the project and, if so, to estimate the cost.

### Bills of quantities (where appropriate)

As discussed in Chapter 4, these list the numbers of all measurable unit quantities required for the completion of each part of a civil or building project, or part of a project. The Contractor can then estimate by applying the unit rates that have been calculated.

## Select Contractors for Invitation

As with estimating, much depends at this stage on historical information about contractors, based on the Owner's own experience, or what has been heard on the grapevine. It is likely that a Contractor's reputation will be based on five aspects of his dealings with clients, all of which the Owner should take into account in making the selection.

### Technical competence

This heading is self-explanatory.

### Compliance with specifications

It is possible to envisage a technically competent job which nevertheless does not conform with the specifications prescribed by the Owner and the Consultant. This would be unsatisfactory to the Owner. For example, concrete evidently perfectly placed in perfect form-work might nevertheless have the wrong mix. A contractor known to cut corners is not to be recommended.

## *Correction of faults*

Although the conditions of contract may be quite clear about the procedures to be followed when either the Owner or Contractor are at fault, a contractor may have a reputation for being reluctant to comply with such procedures.

## *Programme performance*

A contractor should be noted for keeping as closely as possible to agreed schedules of work, and for adapting expeditiously to unexpected circumstances (see Chapter 10).

## *Claims*

Many contracts are of the lump sum type (see Chapter 6). Extra money may legitimately be due to a contractor, when faced with the unexpected, but excessive numbers of claims will be disputed by the Owner, with at least some waste of effort.

## Meeting of Contractors

In addition to allowing interested contractors to question the Owner on matters that are not entirely clear in relation to the project, the meeting of contractors may be of advantage to the Owner in giving advance warning of inconsistencies or omissions in the specifications, and of any unanticipated difficulties. Like the conditions of tender, the meeting should reassure intending bidders that they will be given fair treatment.

## Evaluation of Tenders

It is convenient to consider each tender under five headings, as set out below, and to select the Contractor who not only justified invitation in the first place, but demonstrates worthiness especially in relation to the present project. There is little that can be said in general terms under these five headings, as technical details of a particular project are deeply involved. Some interesting examples are given by Peters (1981).

1 Understanding the nature of the project.
2 Soundness of approach.
3 Compliance with specifications.
4 Previous experience of this kind of work.
5 Managerial staff sufficient in numbers and capability.

Clearly, there is more to awarding a contract than simply selecting the Contractor with the lowest bid.

## Award of Contract

From the time of initiation of the project, the Owner will probably have had in mind the type of contract that it will be appropriate to award on the basis of price and the criteria listed above. Broadly, the choice is from the main types as discussed in Chapter 6, but in the light of work that has already been done, the Owner may expect variations of detail of the contract that are beyond the scope of this discussion. They may well call for professional legal advice.

### Exercises

1 Imagine you are a manufacturing company wishing to build a new factory in a region with which you are not familiar. To bring employment to the area you wish to select your main Contractor locally. Having studied the various check lists in Chapter 5, give, in your own words, an account of the enquiries you would make before selecting contractors for invitation to tender.

2 Search the national and local press, and elsewhere, for examples of projects where it is suggested that

   (a) the main Contractor has done well to overcome unexpected difficulties;

   (b) the Contractor has not shown up well in relation to any of the criteria listed in Chapter 5.

Take care to respect as confidential any inside information you may be able to collect about a real project.

# Part II

# Owner and Main Contractor

# Chapter 6

# Types of Contract

The subject of the contract between the Owner and the main Contractor is very much a matter for the legal profession. In this chapter we can do little more than mention the main types of contract. Some of the problems about which the parties may require to seek legal advice are discussed in Chapter 7. Even when the contract is based on standard procedures and general conditions published by one or group of the professional institutions, legal advice is likely to be sought on particular problems of a project, and any special conditions of contract. Wallace (1978) reveals that the commonly used standard conditions are very far from water-tight.

The classification of projects suggested in Chapter 1 is based on the technical aspects. It is possible to add contractual aspects of the project to the classification, as in Figure 4, which may be compared, for example, with the notes by Hackney (1965:p263). It will be seen that the terminology for types of contract in this and other references is not entirely standardised.

The contract is a working document. It is referred to on a day-to-day basis for deciding courses of action, especially when the progress of the project is not quite straightforward. It includes details of the important procedure whereby the Owner pays the Contractor. A selection of other topics from the conditions of contract are discussed in Chapter 7. Before proceeding, a number of comments must be made on Figure 4.

When a project is very well defined, as with a mechanical process plant with few innovations, where it is certain what machines will be installed, what buildings they will occupy and how they will be arranged on the shop floor, a lump sum or fixed price contract is usual. The sum is specified in the contract and can be altered only if a proven need for variations arises or the Contractor makes a legitimate claim for unanticipated work. Extra money for these must be negotiated as they occur.

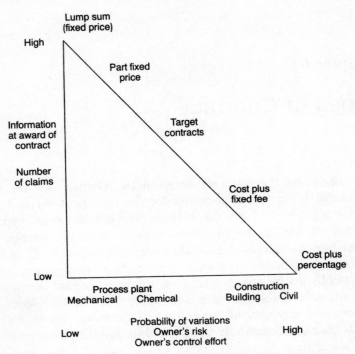

*Figure 4*   Types of contract in relation to the main classes of projects

At the other extreme of definition, a civil engineering project in a remote and geographically difficult area may require a cost-plus or reimbursible contract. When there are so many uncertainties regarding the terrain, labour and transport, for example, no Contractor, or Owner, can be expected to make an accurate enough estimate of costs for a figure to be put in the contract. Thus, the contract must be awarded on the basis that the Contractor will receive the actual costs for the work done. To that will be added a percentage, or a fixed fee, or a sum to be calculated as specified in the contract. A poorly defined project where time or cost is nevertheless of the essence may be the subject of some kind of target cost-plus contract (see below).

In the real world there are projects that lie somewhere in the spectrum between the extremes of lump sum and cost-plus. Figure 4 shows a sliding scale from cost-plus to lump sum in relation to the rough classification of project by type. That there is a degree of over-simplification here may be illustrated by the fact that a small and simple civil engineering contract may well be awarded on a lump sum basis. On the other hand, a mechanical process plant involving activity in an area of high technology, where it is not certain that the process can be run satisfactorily and the product made to specifications within the time scale allotted, might be the subject of a cost-plus contract.

For their respective businesses to prosper, an Owner and a main Contractor have some general objectives in relation to the project. The Owner is looking for good quality of work at as low a cost as is consistent with the definition of the project. As with consumer products, there is little virtue in paying for anything that is not required (i.e. that is outwith the sanctioned definition). The main Contractor, however, looks for a good profit, with minimum risk, together with enhancement of his reputation. The Contractor's future depends on receiving more invitations to tender for contracts. Thus, the question of the Contractor's tender price, or the formula for a cost-plus payment, is a matter of some delicacy for both the Owner and Contractor.

In general, a lump sum contract has advantages for the Owner. Insofar as the Owner's and the Contractor's interests are always somewhat in conflict, some of these advantages to the Owner constitute disadvantages to the Contractor.

(a)  Contractors are put into a competitive situation with respect to each other, and not only as regards price (see Chapter 5).
(b)  In agreeing the lump sum, the Contractor may become involved in some design of the project before work starts, with benefit to the Owner.
(c)  The Owner knows the cost in advance and so knows what funds must be made available and when.
(d)  The nature of the contract requires from the Owner a disciplined approach to definition and specification, if he is not to receive excessive claims for unexpected variations. Disputing claims can lead to expensive litigation.
(e)  The Contractor has a strong incentive to employ the best resources of staff and equipment, as the Contractor will bear the cost of mistakes and over-runs.
(f)  An incompetent Contractor is unlikely to show interest in a project on these terms.
(g)  Little effort on the part of the Owner is required for controlling the project. The onus is chiefly on the Contractor (see (e) above).

In circumstances where a Contractor cannot be found to undertake the work except on a cost-plus basis, the Owner, or the Engineer, will have to keep a closer watch on the project than with a lump sum contract. The price to be paid by the Owner is not stated in the contract, but only the way in which it is to be calculated. Thus, the Contractor is in effect insured against the consequences of uncertainties of several kinds, to the possible disadvantage of the Owner:

(a) Poor definition and specification by the Owner.
(b) Unforeseen difficulties of access, or of statutory requirements, related to the geography of the site.
(c) Unknown or untried aspects of technical innovations.
(d) The state of inflation in the economy (although a fixed price contract should contain clauses to allow for this).
(e) Industrial disputes, that may or may not arise from special features of the particular project.

Figure 4 shows some of the many forms of contract between cost-plus and lump sum. At the cost-plus end of the spectrum, and to ensure that the work is carried out to the satisfaction of both the Owner and the Contractor, it is possible to set up target contracts, based on either the final total cost (to the Contractor), or on the completion date of the project. The contract will include details of how the calculations are to be made, if necessary using graphs or formulae.

Figures 5 and 6 illustrate in a simple way some of the many possibilities. As these diagrams are assumed to have been drawn at the time of the contract, before any costs (except estimating and legal costs) have been incurred by the Contractor, difference between the price asked and the Contractor's costs is referred to as the mark-up, rather than the contribution.

Figure 5 compares a fixed fee contract with two cases of target cost contracts. The cost to the Owner is the price asked by the Contractor. The line at 45° through the origin corresponds to zero mark-up. The line parallel to it indicates a fixed fee, independent of the total cost. If a target fee line is drawn, at less than 45°, through the point defined by the target cost and the fixed fee line, it can be seen that when the Contractor's costs are less than the target, the Owner pays less and the Contractor gets a bonus in excess of the otherwise fixed fee.

If, however, the Contractor's costs exceed the target amount, the Owner pays less than he or she would with a fixed fee, and the

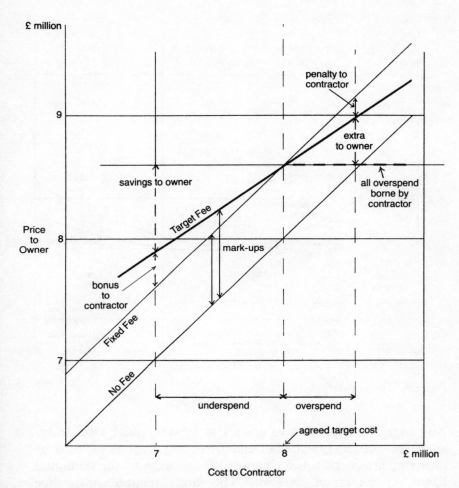

*Figure 5* Target cost contracts

Contractor pays a penalty for overspending. The target fee line encourages the Contractor to keep below the target cost, but does not absolve the Owner from the need to exercise some control of the project, to accommodate some of the cost of an over-run.

In exceptional circumstances the Owner may wish to set a maximum on the price payable. Any overspending by the Contractor then returns the contract to a lump sum type. This is shown by the horizontal line in Figure 5.

Figure 6 shows another way of encouraging the Contractor to give the best, with emphasis now on the completion date. The actual cost will be a minimum for some target completion date.

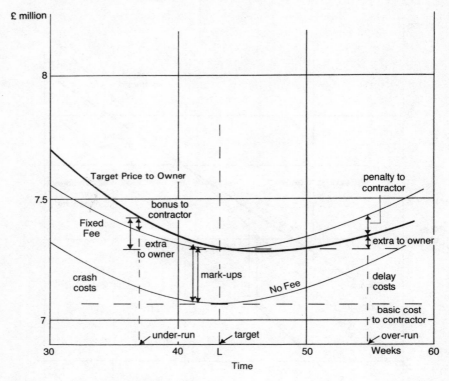

*Figure 6* Target duration contracts

Any over-run implies extra costs (for labour, plant hire, insurance, for example), whilst an under-run may be possible only by incurring crash costs (see Chapter 10) in excess of the minimum based on the target duration. The target reimbursement line therefore has a greater slope than the fixed fee line before the target completion date and a lesser slope beyond. This can be seen to have the effect that the Contractor gets a bonus for early completion and pays a penalty for over-run. It can also be seen that the Owner pays more than the minimum for either an over-run or an under-run.

Some detailed discussion of target contracts is given in Perry & Thompson (1978).

Where payment to the Contractor is based on unit rates for work done, and where there may be doubt concerning the BOQs shown in the specifications, a contract for a civil or building project must include both the agreed unit rates and the method of measurement of quantities (admeasurement). Reference has already been made to standard procedures for this for civil engineering projects (ICE 1985). With a contract running for some years, the allowed costs reached from these calculations may be overtaken by inflation. A possible way of dealing with this is discussed in Chapter 11.

---

### Exercises

1   Exercises 2.3 and 5.2 asked for discussion of some projects actually in progress, or completed. In each case, consider what type of contract would have been used between the Owner and the Main Contractor. If possible, find out, in general terms, what type of contract was in fact used.

2   The question of claims in relation to a lump sum contract is a sensitive one. Some claims are quite straight forward, and agreed amicably between the Owner and the Contractor. Approach one or two local contractors with a view to enquiring, in a low key manner, if they would give some information about claims they have made that lie in this category, i.e. have not involved any protracted negotiating or litigation.

# Chapter 7

# Contract Documents

Although the Contract has been mentioned many times, and referred to as a 'working document', these documents constituting the Contract have not so far been listed. This is another matter in which generalisation is extremely difficult. As an illustration, Figure 7 shows, amongst other things, a typical list of documents. It has been taken from Appendix 1 of the General Conditions of Contract for lump sum contracts for process plants published by the Institution of Chemical Engineers (1976). Analogous examples may be found for reimbursable process plant contracts (IChemE 1981); for mechanical and electrical projects (IMechE 1982); and for civil engineering works (ICE 1973).

The need for standardised General Conditions of Contract, to reduce the chance of error by omission, and to avoid the possibility of wasting time by re-inventing the wheel, is widely acknowledged. Much of what is published in the sets of standard Conditions has been tested in practice, but it seems that they are still legally imperfect in many ways. ICE (1973) the subject of very extensive professional legal comment (Wallace 1978).

Many of the illustrations of project management in this book, especially those in Chapter 10, are taken from civil engineering. To broaden the picture this chapter will refer mainly to chemical engineering plant.

Figure 7 shows a Form of Agreement that serves both to define a number of aspects of the project and to provide a major check list of documents. It names the project; states the name of the Owner and his willingness to have the project carried out; names The Engineer; and names the Contractor and his willingness and ability to do the work. The Form of Agreement lists all those papers that constitute the Contract, the working document, from which day-to-day instructions for the work are taken, as well as those containing the procedures to be followed in the event of problems or disputes. In the Form of Agreement shown, a price is

This Agreement is made the ..................day of.............................19..............
between....................................................... of..........................................................
(hereinafter called "the Purchaser") of the one part and
........................................................................ of..........................................................
(hereinafter called "the Contractor") of the other part.

*WHEREAS*

1. The Purchaser wishes to have a process plant to be known as ...........................
...................................................... at.......................................
   and to this end wishes the Contractor to complete the design of and to execute and complete the Works (as hereinafter defined).

2. The Contractor is able to complete such design and to execute and complete the Works for the consideration and upon the terms hereafter appearing.

*NOW THIS AGREEMENT* provides as follows:

1. The following documents only and their annexes, if any, shall together constitute the Contract between the Purchaser and the Contractor and the term "the Contract" shall in all such documents be construed accordingly.

   (a) this Form of Agreement
   (b) the General Conditions of Contract
   (c) the Special Conditions (if any)
   (d) the Specification and Drawings (if any) listed therein or annexed thereto
   (e) the following Schedules

   Schedule 1 Description of Works     Schedule 5 Take-over Procedures
   Schedule 2 Drawings for Approval     Schedule 6 Performance Tests
   Schedule 3 Final Drawings and        Schedule 7 Payment of the
               Manuals                       Contract Price
   Schedule 4 Time and Stages of       Schedule 8 Liquidated Damages
               Completion

          Part I for Delay
          Part II for Failure of Performance Tests

   For the purpose of identification the said Conditions, Specification and Schedules are bound together with this Form of Agreement and have been signed on behalf of the Purchaser and the Contractor.

2. The Contract as hereinbefore defined constitutes a full statement of the contractual rights and liabilities of the Purchaser and the Contractor in relation to the Works and no negotiations between them nor any document agreed or signed by them prior to the date of the Contract in relation to the Works shall hereafter be of any contractual effect.

3. The Contract price is the sum of £ ..............................................................
   (...........................................................................................................)

4. For all purposes of the Contract the date of the Contractor's Tender shall be the.........................................................................................19.............
   and the date of the Purchaser's acceptance therefore shall be the
   ...................................................................................................19..............

5. Subject to Clause 10(The Engineer) of the General Conditions of Contract, the Purchaser hereby appoints ...........................................................................
   ........................................................ of ....................................................

   *IN WITNESS* whereof the parties hereto have caused this Agreement to be signed by their duly authorised officers or representatives on the date first above written.

*Figure 7* A form of Agreement

stated. For a reimbursable (cost-plus) contract, the price would be replaced with procedures and formulae for calculation of a price.

There should be a programme of work in the Contract (Schedule 4), usually prepared by the Contractor, and approved by the Engineer. (The use of the word 'schedule' with two quite different meanings in this chapter is unfortunate, but must be accepted as common usage.) The programme should include copies of activity networks and bar charts, which are helpful in defining responsibilities as well as making clear a schedule of activities for the Contractor (see Chapter 10).

The various Schedules mentioned in the Form of Agreement are specific to a project, and cannot easily be standardised. A possible exception is Schedule 7, Payment of the Contract Price. Procedures for payment, in general terms, are already the subject of Condition 39, but Schedule 7 must be specific about the frequency of instalments, and also the matter of 'retentions'. Retentions are amounts withheld from the Contractor, perhaps 3%, 5% or even 10% of the amount due, as a kind of insurance for the Owner against poor workmanship. All these payments are subject to certification by the Engineer of work satisfactorily completed and the proper admeasurement of those parts of the project where an accurate bill of quantities could not be drawn up in advance.

It is very important to note that the General Conditions refer frequently to the Schedules, and therefore a number of the Conditions are meaningless without them. Taken together, the Conditions and the Schedules define the division of responsibility for the project between the Owner and the Contractor in such a way as to advance the project to their mutual advantage and to obviate, as far as possible, any need for litigation in settling disputes.

The document from which Figure 7 is taken is commonly known, for obvious reasons, as The Red Book (its companion volume, for reimbursable contracts, is known as The Green Book). The following, arbitrary, selection from the Conditions is intended to give examples of aspects of project management that are commonly held to be troublesome.

The Conditions have 47 clauses, beginning with definitions, and matters of interpretation. For example, 'The contract shall be governed and construed according to the laws of England'. In the event of conflicts of provision, the Schedules shall take precedence over the Special Conditions; and these shall take precedence over the General Conditions. 'No approval or consent required to be obtained under the contract shall be unreasonably refused by either party.'

The Contractor shall adopt sound workmanship and materials, according to good engineering practice, and to the reasonable satisfaction of the Engineer 'the plant...shall be in every respect suitable for the purposes for which it is intended'.

The Owner must ensure that facilities, services and information are provided to enable the Contractor to proceed according to the Contract, and without contravening the law of the land in any way.

Many of the clauses in the Conditions relate to communication, especially between the Owner and the Engineer, the Engineer and the Contractor, and between the Contractor and the sub-contractors, with a statement of the time within which any formal communication, usually written, must be made. There are examples related to many aspects of the project.

The Contractor usually nominates a sub-contractor, but the Contract may allow the Engineer to do this. If the Contractor foresees problems with the Engineer's sub-contractor, then the Contractor must notify the Engineer within 28 days of the nomination.

The Contractor shall report progress on the project to the Engineer 'at intervals of not more than 31 days', at a site meeting where minutes are taken and circulated within seven days. The Owner may appoint a new Engineer, but must notify the Contractor within seven days of the new appointment.

There are clauses concerned with site working conditions, site services, insurance, ownership of materials, copyright of drawings, mistakes in drawings, inspection, and clearance of the site when the work is completed. Provision is made for dealing with default on the part of the Contractor and termination of the work on the part of the Owner. A list of circumstances (some of which will be familiar to anyone with a household insurance policy—earthquake, civil commotion, for example) is provided under the heading of force majeure, any of which excuse a party from compliance with the Contract. After 120 days of enforced inactivity, the Contract may be terminated without penalty either way.

The titles of the Schedules listed in Figure 7 are self-explanatory in general terms. To assist in their effective preparation, the Conditions of Contract include detailed guidance. At about 30 points in these notes there is mention of the possible need for

Special Conditions of Contract to be written. The Special Conditions may then be collected together, as indicated on the form. As with the General Conditions, they may have little meaning without reference to the Schedules.

## Exercises

1 Write a short essay on the advantages and disadvantages of making use of model conditions of contract in relation to a capital project.

2 Study the different model conditions of contracts drawn up by the civil, chemical, electrical, and mechanical engineers, and comment on the differences found amongst them.

# Part III
# Main Contractor

# Chapter 8

# Contractor's Cash Flows

In the documents described in Chapters 5 and 7 details are given of the procedures by which the Contractor will be paid by the Owner for work done. Payments from the Owner are likely to be monthly, in arrears, and will not in any case be the full price for the work done, because of retentions. The Contractor, on the other hand, will have to pay for labour, materials, plant hire, and sub-contractors, on a weekly or monthly basis, with cash in excess of that already received from the Owner. As with receipts from the Owner, some of these payments, for example for materials, may be due a month in arrears. Wages, however, will be payable weekly. In addition to estimating the cost of the whole project, to enable the Contractor to arrive at a realistic price to ask of the Owner, the Contractor must also ask at the time of putting in a bid: what will be the financial position during the course of a contract? As with some cost estimating procedures (see Chapter 4), it is necessary to look at as much historical information as possible before attempting to answer the question.

Experience of previous projects will have shown the Contractor that the value of the work done usually varies cumulatively with time in the manner of the S-curve shown in Figure 8 (Harris & McCaffer 1983). Such a standard curve, with units on both axes as a percentage, of total cumulative value and of total duration, may in principle be established using data from a large number of projects of the same type but of different durations and total values. It can then be used for a new project, by translating the units on the axes into actual cumulative value and actual time. In practice, and again like estimating, it is unlikely that adequate historical data can be found, so human judgement will play an important part in setting up an S-curve for predicting cash flows. (For the S-curve for project control purposes see Chapter 11.)

The calculations that follow in this chapter are appropriate for evaluation of a capital project by the Contractor. The Owner, as

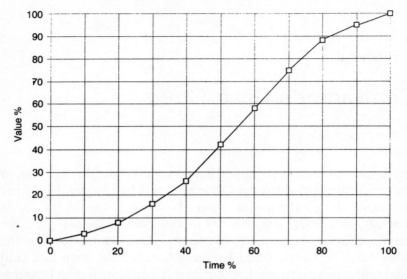

*Figure 8* Standard S-curve: percentage value against percentage elapsed time

seen for example in Figure 2, may wish to predict cash flows for the project as a whole over a period of years, including the operation of the facility that is being built. Running expenses, revenue from sales, taxation and rates of interest after completion of the work then have to be considered. Payments to the Contractor represent only one aspect of the project for the Owner. Complete evaluation of the project from the Owner's point of view is a subject for study in itself outside the scope of this book.

As the duration of the Contractor's contribution to the project is likely to be much less than that of the Owner's involvement, questions of discounting and inflation will not be introduced as they are unimportant on the shorter time scale (but see Chapter 11). Taxation, an aspect depending very much on the Contractor's overall financial position, is more a matter for professional accountants, and this also is beyond the scope of this chapter.

It is not difficult to see that S-curves such as the one in Figure 8 give a reasonable summary of progress in the construction work of a project. At the start, work proceeds slowly, for example whilst the site is being cleared and materials are on order. Then progress picks up for a time while the major activities take place. Towards the end many small jobs have to be done to finish off the project, without adding much to the value which is now approaching its plateau. At the plateau, the value shown on the S-curve is in fact equal to the Contractor's estimate, plus the mark-up. (Remember that these calculations are being done before the contract has been awarded and any work done.)

The cumulative nature of the S-curve, and of the calculations derived from it, is useful for several reasons. The cash flow at a month end is the difference so far between the total in and the total out. When the project is under way, and control procedures are in operation (see Chapter 11), the cumulative method is a convenient way of incorporating some of the arithmetic that has to be done somewhere. Again with reference to Chapter 11, the work and costs for any one month are most easily found by comparing the cumulative status at this month end with the status at last month end.

From the total value, the total duration and the shape of the S-curve the Contractor can investigate the cash flows for the project. A simple example will show the procedure, but it will be clear that there are many ways in which details could be different in practice. Suppose a Contractor has been awarded a contract of value £3.5 million. This is the Contractor's estimate of the cost (to him) plus a mark-up of, say, 15%. The project will take 18 months to complete. The Contractor expects the value to grow with time as shown in Figure 9, which has the same shape as the curve in Figure 8, but with scales now in months and £million respectively.

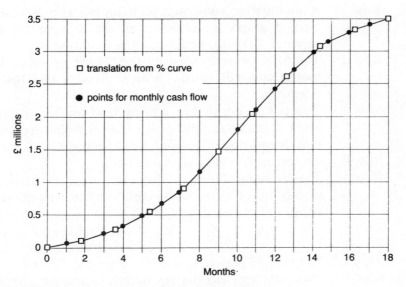

*Figure 9* S-curve: actual value against elapsed time

For purposes of clearer illustration, detailed calculations will be given for a project of less realistic duration.

Consider a project worth £250 000 to the Contractor. The work will take 5 months. From an appropriate S-curve, the value is expected to increase with time as shown as project value near the top of Figure 10. The costs comprise 25% for labour, 40% for materials and 35% for plant hire. Labour costs are payable at the end of each month in which the work is done; materials and plant hire charges are paid for one month in arrears. The Contractor wins the project with a mark-up of 15%.

Reimbursement will also be one month in arrears, less 10% retention, with the total retention payable at the end of the second month following completion of the project.

If the Contractor should need a loan for the duration of this project, interest will be payable monthly at a rate of 24% per annum, not in arrears.

The calculations are best set out on a spread sheet as in Figure 10, where some rows are numbered for quick reference. Receipts are sums paid to the Contractor; payments are sums paid by the Contractor. All the rows are treated cumulatively, following the pattern of the S-curve. For these calculations it is assumed that the project will go according to plan, with certification of work satisfactorily completed at each month end.

Row 1    A cumulative value for each month end is read from a graph translated from the S-curve for a value of £250 000 and 5 months' duration.

Row 2    The total of cash owed by the Owner up to each month end will be the value in Row 1, less 10% retention.

Row 3    This is the sum in row 2 being paid one month in arrears, i.e. at the end of the month following the month end when the value was checked.

Row 4    The retentions are eventually paid.

Row 5    The estimated cost to the Contractor is conveniently incorporated in the table as a function of the value and the mark-up.

Row 6    The cost of labour is 25% of the total cost.

Row 7    Labour is paid at the end of the current month.

Row 8    The cost of materials is 40% of the total cost.

Row 9    Materials are paid for one month in arrears.

Row 10   The cost of plant hire is 35% of the total cost.

Value is value to the Contractor
Cost is cost to the Contractor
A receipt is cash received by the Contractor
A payment is cash paid by the Contractor

All sums in the tabulation are in £'000's
Each row gives a cumulative quantity (except row 15)

Mark-up     = 15% of estimate      Materials cost   = 40% of total cost
Retention   = 10% of value         Plant hire cost  = 35% of total cost
Labour cost = 25% of total cost    Rate of interest = 24% per annum

| | MONTH ENDS | 0 | 1 | 2 | 3 | 4 | 5 | 6 | 7 |
|---|---|---|---|---|---|---|---|---|---|
| 1 | Project value | 0 | 42 | 107 | 179 | 228 | 250 | 250 | 250 |
| 2 | Value less 10% retention | | 37.8 | 96.3 | 161.1 | 205.2 | 225.0 | 225.0 | 225.0 |
| [3] | Receipts for work done | 0 | 0.0 | 37.8 | 96.3 | 161.1 | 205.2 | 225.0 | 225.0 |
| [4] | Receipts from retentions | | | | | | | | 25.0 |
| 5 | Total cost so far [value/(1 + mark up)] | 0 | 36.5 | 93.0 | 155.7 | 198.3 | 217.4 | 217.4 | 217.4 |
| 6 | Labour cost 25% | | 9.1 | 23.3 | 38.9 | 49.6 | 54.3 | 54.3 | 54.3 |
| [7] | Labour payment | | 9.1 | 23.3 | 38.9 | 49.6 | 54.3 | 54.3 | 54.3 |
| 8 | Materials cost 40% | | 14.6 | 37.2 | 62.3 | 29.3 | 87.0 | 87.0 | 87.0 |
| [9] | Materials payment | | | 14.6 | 37.2 | 62.3 | 79.3 | 87.0 | 87.0 |
| 10 | Plant hire cost 35% | | 12.8 | 32.6 | 54.5 | 69.4 | 76.1 | 76.1 | 76.1 |
| [11] | Plant hire payment | | | 12.8 | 32.6 | 54.5 | 69.4 | 76.1 | 76.1 |
| 12 | Cash flow ([3] + [4] − [7] − [9] − [11]) | | − 9.1 | − 12.9 | − 12.4 | − 5.2 | 2.2 | 7.6 | 32.6 |
| [13] | Loan received | 10 | 10 | 10 | 10 | 10 | 10 | 10 | 10 |
| [14] | Loan paid back | | | | | | | | 10 |
| 15 | Interest per month | | 0.2 | | | | | | |
| [16] | Interest payment | | 0.2 | 0.4 | 0.6 | 0.8 | 1.0 | 1.2 | 1.4 |
| 17 | Cash flow with loan ({[3] + [4] − [7] − [9] − [11] + [13] − [14] − [16]) | | 0.7 | − 3.3 | − 3.0 | 4.0 | 11.2 | 16.4 | 31.2 |

The loan reduces the maximum overdraft from £12 900 to £3300 but also reduces the hoped for contribution from £32 600 to £31 200.

*Figure 10*   Analysis of project cash flow for the Contractor

Row 11 Plant hire is paid for one month in arrears.
Row 12 For each month end addition of the rows where cash has actually changed hands gives the cash flow.

When the cash flows are plotted, as in Figure 11 (upper curve) it becomes very clear that a mark-up will be converted fully into a contribution to profit and overheads only at the very end of the work. Up to that time, the project must be financed from the Contractor's own resources. If the Contractor has many projects running, then those just completed may be a source of funds for those in progress. Otherwise a loan may be required, from the bank perhaps. As interest will have to be paid on the loan, the ultimate contribution will be somewhat reduced. This effect is shown in the final rows of the calculation for a loan of £10 000, and in the lower curve of Figure 11.

Row 13 Loan taken up.
Row 14 Loan paid back.
Row 15 Interest payments.
Row 16 Cash flow with loan.

Assuming that the loan is taken up at the end of month 0 (i.e. at

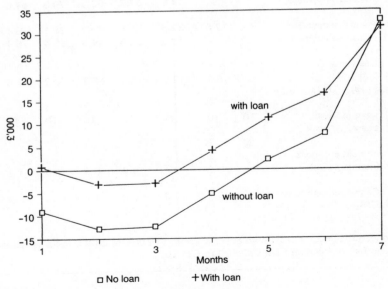

*Figure 11* Project cash flows with and without a loan

the beginning of month 1) and not repaid until the end of month 7, then the loss of contribution will be £1400.

The data used in the above example have been kept simple for the purposes of illustration. In particular, the figure of 10% for retentions is higher than would be expected in real life, especially for a much larger project, where 3% might be more usual. It may be noticed that the loan could in fact have been paid back at little more than half-way to completion. More subtle handling of the loan would be expected with a very large project.

The calculations discussed above are very much Contractor oriented. The reader is reminded that there has been no mention of inflation, discounting, or taxation. Inflation might not be important in a project lasting only 5 months, but taxation would certainly have to be considered. A further complication arises in relation to the Contractor's operations as a whole. Certain sums may have to be set aside to pay dividends to shareholders. All these are matters for the attention of professional accountants.

The Owner's likely interest in discounted cash flows for the project as a whole was touched on above. Some justification for neglecting this aspect from the Contractor's point of view is given in Figure 12, where the cash flows from Figure 10 have been reduced to monthly values and discounted back to the start of the project to get present values (PVs). The mark-up has also been discounted back, as if it were a single payment at completion. The differences among the PVs are small.

| | | | | | | | |
|---|---|---|---|---|---|---|---|
| Cumulative cash flow—no loan | − 9.1 | − 12.9 | − 12.4 | − 5.2 | 2.2 | 7.6 | 32.6 |
| Monthly cash flow | | − 9.1 | − 3.7 | 0.5 | 7.2 | 7.4 | 5.5 | 25.0 |
| PV @ 24% p.a.  = £27.82 | | | | | | | |
| | | | | | | | |
| PV of contribution | | | | | | | |
| as a single payment = £25.09 | | | | | | Contribution = £32.61 | |
| − no loan | | | | | | | |
| | | | | | | | |
| Cumulative cash flow with loan | 0.7 | − 3.3 | − 3.0 | 4.0 | 11.2 | 16.4 | 31.2 |
| Monthly cash flow | 0.7 | − 3.9 | 0.3 | 7.0 | 7.2 | 5.3 | 14.8 |
| PV @ 24% p.a. = £27.62 | | | | | | | |
| | | | | | | | |
| PV of contribution | | | | | | | |
| as a single payment = £24.01 | | | | | | Contribution = £31.21 | |

*Figure 12* PV of monthly cash flows and of the contribution as a single payment

## Exercises

1   A Contractor has won a project worth £500000 fixed price, with a mark-up as high as 25% because of expertise to get the work done quickly (in 10 months, as against the best competitor's estimate of 15 months). However, the Contractor's bank manager will be unhappy with any overdraft from the project exceeding a few hundred pounds, unless an arrangement is made in advance. That would mean a short term loan, with interest at 1.8% per month.

The value of work done is expected to follow the S-curve shown in Figure 13, whilst costs are made up throughout the work from 30% labour, paid at the end of the month; and 70% materials, paid one month in arrears. The value of certificated work done, less 10% retentions, is received one month in arrears. Retentions will be received three months after completion. Find:

   (a) The cash flows from the project without a loan.
   (b) The value of the loan, to the nearest £5000, that you think the Contractor will have to borrow.

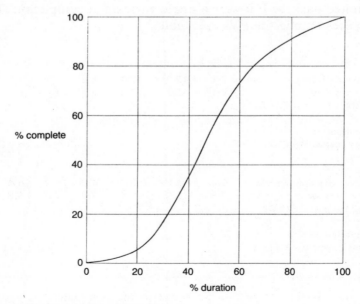

*Figure 13*   S-curve for exercise 1

(c) The earliest month end on which it will be possible to pay off the loan.

(d) The overall contribution to overheads and profit expected from the project.

2   A Contractor undertakes to build and equip a small high technology process plant, of a type built before. The building will take 6 months and have a value of £200 000,

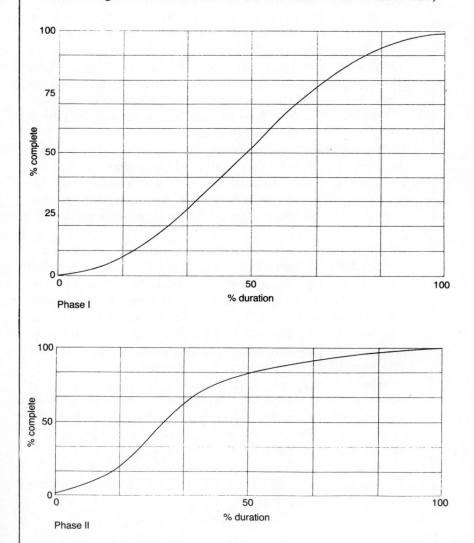

Phase I

Phase II

*Figure 14*   S-curves for exercise 2

including a mark-up of 12%. Installing the equipment will take another 3 months. With the same percentage mark-up, the equipment will have a value of £1.2 million. The Contractor expects the cumulative value of the two non-overlapping phases to follow the patterns shown in Figure 14.

For Phase I, labour costs are 50% of total costs, payable monthly. Materials, also half of total costs, are payable 1 month in arrears. For Phase II, 5% of costs are for labour, payable monthly; 10% for materials and 85% for equipment, both payable 1 month in arrears. Certificated work in Phase I yields reimbursements one month in arrears, less 5% retention payable on completion of Phase II. Also in Phase II, reimbursements are 1 month in arrears, but less 10% retentions payable 2 months after completion of the project.

Calculate the cash flow to the Contractor for the period up to receipt of the final retention.

If the Contractor cannot sustain the negative cash flows, investigate the effect on overall profit of borrowing £20 000 at the start, with interest at 20% per annum, payable quarterly. The loan is to be repaid, together with the last month's interest, on receipt of the last retention payment.

3   A Contractor has been awarded a contract of estimated value £250 000, comprising costs plus 15% mark-up. It will take 15 months (5 quarters) to complete the work. The Contractor's costs will be made up of 60% for labour and 40% for materials, the payments for labour being made at the end of each quarter; and for materials one quarter in arrears. No sub-contractors are involved, but an overhead payment of £5000 per quarter is payable to a Consulting Engineer at the end of each quarter in which work is in progress. Interim receipts from the Owner, following certification, will be made one quarter in arrears, subject to retentions of 5%. Retentions will be payable, all going well, six months from completion of the work.

Using the S-curve of Figure 8 as a basis, show how the Contractor's cash flow from this project varies through the duration of the project.

# Chapter 9

# Competitive Bidding for Contracts

Chapter 5 dealt with procedures followed by the Owner in putting a contract out to tender, written from the point of view of the Owner. It was assumed that selected contractors would receive the tender documents. Having studied them, some contractors (perhaps all) would wish to proceed with a bid for the contract. Each contractor would carry out an estimation of the cost (see Chapter 4) based on the information provided in the documents, anything else learned at the contractors' meeting and personal experience and knowledge. Starting with the more sophisticated of the methods discussed in Chapter 4, the Contractor would supplement these with historical information from previous contracts and any special techniques derived from inside experience as a contractor. Estimation to the degree of accuracy desirable before bidding for a contract is notoriously difficult and as will be seen below, the success of a contractor's business may well depend on some estimates being too low and some too high. Without good accuracy of estimate, choosing a winning value for the mark-up is more of a lottery than it need be.

However accurate the estimate may be, choosing a mark-up is still very much a matter of judgement. If it is too high, the Contractor is unlikely to win the contract, unless there are no other bidders. If the mark-up is too low, the Contractor may win, but the eventual contribution will be small, or even negative.

Although tender price is not the only criterion by which a bid is judged, it usually plays a major part in the Owner's decision as to whom the contract will be awarded. If the tender price only is significant, the Owner might as well treat the bids as sealed and award the contract to the lowest one opened, without taking into account the other aspects listed in Chapter 5. This would be rather like placing a sealed bid for house purchase, as commonly practised in Scotland, but of course there the property goes to the highest bidder.

For bids that are not extreme, the Contractor is interested in the probability of winning. This is an important question, because the Contractor must aim to strike a balance between taking on more work than perhaps can be managed and taking on less than is needed to continue successfully in business. In addition the Contractor must be fully aware that the estimate is liable to be inaccurate. At the bidding stage, prices and costs are more or less hypothetical:

tender price = estimate + mark-up

On completion of the project, the equation becomes, for a fixed price contract, and omitting the matter of claims:

value (tender price) = actual cost + contribution

The actual cost to the Contractor may be more or less than the estimate. If it happens to be less, then a contract won with a very low mark-up may yield a good contribution. Conversely, when the actual cost is greater than the estimate, the contribution will be less than the mark-up, so that when the tender price is paid, the contribution may even turn into a loss.

A model of a relationship between estimate and actual cost has been given by Harris & McCaffer (1983) as part of a business game. Harris & McCaffer assume a model in which there is some figure, a likely cost, $C$, unknown to either the Owner or the Contractor, to which the estimate and the actual cost are related by factors, near to unity, on a basis of probability. Probability distributions for the factors are shown in Figure 15, $F_e$ for the estimate, and $F_a$ for the actual cost. The percentage difference, $D$, between the actual cost and the estimate is given by

$$D = \frac{F_a C - F_e C}{F_e C} \times 100 = \frac{F_a - F_e}{F_e} \times 100$$

which can be positive or negative. If $F_e$ is greater than 1, and $F_a$ is less than 1, for example, then the contract could be won with a small mark-up and still give a satisfactory contribution. If on the other hand $F_e$ is much less than $F_a$ the Contractor could be in trouble, unless the contract is won with the large mark-up necessary to compensate for the excessive costs.

The two probability distributions in this model are normal distributions and are entirely notional as it is difficult to see how they could be established in practice. They do however help to illuminate the problem. Their shape is reasonable: both estimate

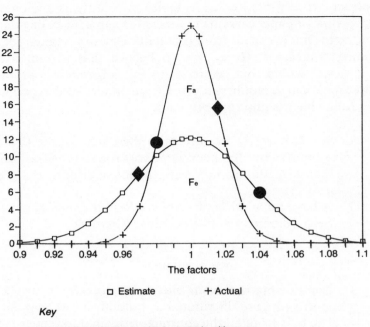

*Figure 15* Factors for estimate and actual cost from 'likely cost' in the bidding game; bidding factors, estimate 0.033, actual 0.016

and actual cost have a high probability of being near to the likely cost, the most probable value of both $F_e$ and $F_a$ being 1.

A number of other mathematical models have been set up with a view to answering the question: what is the relationship between mark-up and the probability of winning the contract? They have been well summarised by Woodward (1975). All the models depend on knowing certain probabilities, and it is by no means clear that this requirement can ever be met in real life. The models' great virtue, like many in management science, is that their construction calls for simplification and analysis of a complicated situation, possibly showing up relationships and consequences that might otherwise have been missed.

The treatment of a bidding situation given below, based on Harris & McCaffer (1983), illustrates the problem. It makes the assumption that the Contractor has no grapevine information, and that, as far as he is concerned, the procedure for awarding the contract, when the criterion is tender price only, is analogous to taking slips of paper carrying numbers $R$ from a black bag that the Contractor has prepared from past data. One slip is taken for each bidding contractor. (It is easy to believe that in real life the Contractor would put more faith in information from the grapevine, than in numbers derived from an idealised experiment.) The following assumptions are made.

1  The Contractor has access to the tender prices that were submitted by all other contractors for all previous projects that were similar in nature, if not in size, to the present project.
2  A large population of numbers $R$ on the slips of paper has been obtained from these bids, where

$$R = \frac{\text{competitor's tender price}}{\text{own estimate}} \times 100$$

3  The $R$s obtained from bids from different projects and contractors are distributed at random in the population.
4  The bids from all the contractors invited to tender for the present contract give $R$ values that belong to this same population.

The Contractor wants guidance in choosing a mark-up. The Contractor knows his estimates, to which a mark-up was added to get a tender price. For any other contractor, only past tender prices are known, not estimates and mark-ups separately. The Contractor therefore prepares the population of numbers by finding the ratio $R$ for all competitors and all previous projects. A histogram of $R$ might appear as in Figure 16a. Given a large enough number of $R$ values, the histogram may be converted into the inverse cumulative probability (ICP) distribution, shown in Figure 16b.

To make an estimate of the probability that the Contractor's bid for a new contract will beat i.e. be lower than, that of any one competitor, the Contractor finds for his own bid a number $R^*$ given by

$$R^* = \frac{\text{own tender price}}{\text{own estimate}} \times 100$$

$$= \frac{\text{own estimate} + \text{mark-up}}{\text{own estimate}} \times 100$$

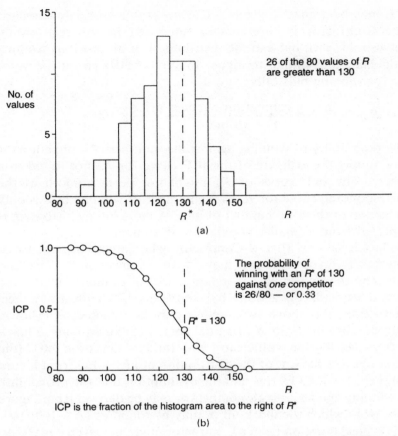

*Figure 16*   (a) Histogram of *R* values; (b) inverse cumulative probability of R values

and locates this value on the *R*-axis of Figure 16b. The Contractor reads off the corresponding ICP.

On the basis of this model, the Contractor looks for $R = R^*$ in Figure 16b. The probability *P* that the Contractor wins against any one competitor is the probability that the competitor's tender price corresponds to an *R* greater than $R^*$. This probability is the fraction of the area under the histogram of Figure 16a to the right of $R^*$. This is equal to the ordinate of the ICP curve at $R = R^*$ in Figure 16b.

The probability of the Contractor winning against *n* competitors, all of whose bids give *R*-values belonging to the same population, is the probability that all their bids are higher than his: viz. $P^n$.

It may be argued that this procedure is unnecessarily complex. The Contractor is surely more interested in the relationship between his own bid and the distribution of all previous winning bids. Diagrams similar to Figure 16 might be drawn for the ratios $R_w$ for winning bids only:

$$R_w = \frac{\text{winning competitor's tender price}}{\text{own estimate}} \times 100$$

The probability of winning against any number of competitors is now simply the ordinate of the ICP curve for $R_w$ not raised to a power. The ICP curve of $R_w$ might not be as smooth as the corresponding curve for $R$, as the number of winning bids is only a fraction of the total number of bids. A more lumpy histogram is expected from a smaller population of numbers.

Thus it is seen that a Contractor who intends to bid for a contract is faced with two main areas of uncertainty. The first concerns the actual cost in relation to the estimate, whilst the second depends on actions by competitors. To illustrate their interaction, the above two models may be adapted as follows. Suppose that the ratio $X$ of actual cost $A$ to the estimate $E$ has a normal distribution with mean 1 and standard deviation 0.037 (the latter figure is the s.d. of the distribution of $(F_a - F_e)$ from Figure 15), i.e. $A = XE$. To this add the assumption that the probability of winning against a single competitor may be derived from Figure 16b, from which the mark-up $m$ may be found as $(R - 100)/100$.

A typical question from a Contractor might be: given a mark-up of $100m\%$, what is the probability $P$ that the contribution will exceed $100c\%$ of the estimate, where $c$ is a chosen fraction? What also is the probability of winning? Thus:

$$P[\text{contribution} > = cE]$$
$$= P[\{E(1 + m) - A\} > = cE]$$
$$= P[\{E(1 + m) - EX\} - cE > = 0]$$
$$= P[1 + m - X - c > = 0]$$

For the case when $100c\% = 10\%$, Table 3 may be drawn up. Column (4) is a value from the standard normal distribution, and column (5) is its cumulative probability.

A Contractor who is invited to bid for a project may choose not to do so, for any of a number of reasons. Taking into account work already in progress on other projects, the Contractor must ask if sufficient resources are available, of all kinds, including cash. Will the Contractor need, and be able to afford, a loan?

TABLE 3

| (1) | (2) | (3) | (4) | (5) | (6) | (7) |
|-----|-----|-----|-----|-----|-----|-----|
| Mark-up % | $m$ | $1 + m - c$ | $\dfrac{\{(3) - 1\}}{0.037}$ | $P[X <= (3)]$ | $P(\text{win})$ 1 comp. | $P(\text{win})$ 4 comp. |
| 0 | 0.00 | 0.90 | − 2.7 | 0.003 | 0.95 | 0.81 |
| 5 | 0.05 | 0.95 | − 1.35 | 0.09 | 0.92 | 0.72 |
| 10 | 0.10 | 1.00 | 0.0 | 0.50 | 0.85 | 0.52 |
| 15 | 0.15 | 1.05 | 1.35 | 0.91 | 0.75 | 0.32 |
| 20 | 0.20 | 1.10 | 2.7 | 0.997 | 0.62 | 0.15 |

With a 15% mark-up, there is a 91% chance of making a 10% contribution, but only a 32% chance of winning the contract with four competitors, on the basis of these models.

Does the project offer a financially attractive prospect? Are there good reasons why the Contractor would not wish to work with this particular Owner anyway? To decline an invitation to bid for a contract is easy, but should be done if at all, in a way that does not antagonise a potential future client.

On the other hand, to bid with a high probability of winning is more difficult. At a time of prosperity, at least for the Contractor, this is not important. The Contractor may then choose freely amongst the contracts on offer, selecting for attention those whose duration and resource requirements are compatible with work already in hand. With these the Contractor can afford to apply modest mark-ups, with their reasonable chance of winning, but without great hopes of spectacular profits.

In times of difficulty, on the other hand, the Contractor may wish to increase the chance of winning, with rather low mark-ups. By sacrificing some profit, for the time being, the Contractor hopes to keep the business running, cover overhead costs, and at the same time build up a reputation. Whilst the Contractor's estimate of cost should be as objective and accurate as possible, the mark-up that is added to it is decided partly, at least, on subjective grounds.

**Exercises**

1  Investigate some of the other bidding models to be found in the literature, and discuss the extent to which they are (a) realistic, and (b) likely to be useful to a Contractor in making decisions.

2  A Contractor believes the estimate made is an accurate estimate of the cost of a project—£1.4 million. If the Contractor wishes to achieve a contribution of £200 000, in the event that the contract is won, what must the mark-up be? Assuming the probability distributions in Figure 16 are applicable to this kind of project, what is the probability that the Contractor will win (a) against one competitor, and (b) against four competitors?

# Chapter 10

# Scheduling the Project

A major technique available to the Contractor for scheduling the project is network analysis. It has evolved over the last 30 years, in different forms and under various names, for example, critical path method (CPM); project evaluation review technique (PERT); critical path analysis (CPA). The essence of the technique is to divide the project into separate activities, each of which represents a significant step towards completion and has a certain logical relationship with all the others.

To control progress of the project as a whole, an individual activity must not itself be so large that it cannot be controlled as an entity; nor must activities be so small that control is frustrated by the sheer complexity of the network. Thus, the mode of sub-division is to some extent a matter of judgement. The activities are represented in their relationships with one another as a network diagram, from which a bar chart may be compiled, as a day-to-day working document, showing the activities against a time scale or calendar.

The network diagram may take one of two general forms, usually reading from left to right. The activities may be represented by arrows, linked by nodes according to the logic of the situation. Nodes indicate the start and finish of each activity. This is an arrow, or $i/j$, diagram. Data concerning the activity may be written along the arrows, which give the diagram a directional character.

Alternatively, the activities may be shown as node boxes, containing activity data, and linked, again according to the logic of the activities, by precedence links. The result is an activity-on-node, or precedence, diagram. Personal preference plays a part in choosing one or the other; each has advantages and disadvantages. As the arrow diagram usually gives a better impression of the flow of a project, at least with small illustrative networks, it will be used in this chapter. In professional work, a precedence diagram might be preferred as it is more adaptable to changing circumstances. The two methods are compared in Appendix 1.

A small project has fewer activities than a large one, and with less than, say, 20 activities the formalities of network analysis may not be worthwhile, except for learning purposes (see below). On the other hand, a large project may consist of thousands, or many thousands, of activities, requiring standardised techniques of great sophistication. Once broken down into activities, the objective is to ensure that the project is completed on time, at lowest cost, taking into account the necessary logical relationships between the activities. Any restrictions on the amounts of resources available at any time must be taken into account. Checking progress of the project in relation to the network and barchart will show how best to plan the work ahead and take contingency action whenever necessary.

Many computing packages are available to aid analysis of the project data. Before attempting to use any of them, it is crucial to learn the principles involved by means of examples of small networks, and to work with pencil and paper. The same small networks may later be analysed with the computing package, thus generating confidence in the method, and in how the package works, to the point where a network that is too large to be treated and checked by hand can safely be given to the machine. This is specially important where there are problems of resource allocation. For present purposes, procedures for working by hand only are given.

Before a start can be made on the diagram, the activities must be listed together with all relevant information.

1 Brief description.
2 A coding symbol.
3 Logical precedents, referred to by code.
4 Expected duration.
5 Names of resources required, and amounts.

It cannot be over emphasised that network analysis is very much a process of iteration and updating. This is why the speed of machine computing is so valuable in large projects. As the diagram takes shape, following the rules, it may become clear that some activities have been omitted; or they are excessively subdivided; or precedents are incorrect; or the layout of the diagram is not as helpful as it might be. Many corrections may be necessary before the final diagram is reached.

As time is of the essence in a project, something must be said about it before proceeding further. Each activity has a duration, but it starts and finishes at instants in time, or events, represented by the nodes. To avoid ambiguity, we adopt the convention that *duration* implies an elapsed time; whilst *time* refers to an instant in time, particularly an event.

## The rules

1   Each arrow must begin and end at a circle carrying the node number, and spaces for an earliest event time (EET) and latest event time (LET). Unless specified to the contrary, these times relate to the finish of an activity (Figure 17a). That is to say, the earliest time that an activity can possibly finish and the latest time that the following one can start without holding up the entire project.

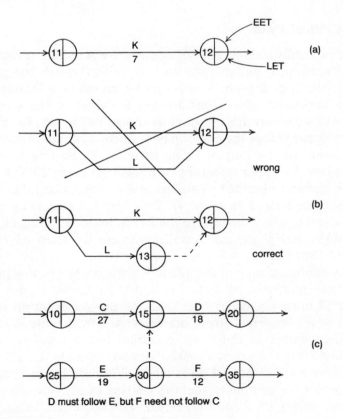

D must follow E, but F need not follow C

*Figure 17*   Elements of an arrow diagram

2  Each arrow must carry a description of the activity, or a coding, and a duration.
3  The entire project must start and finish with a single node at each end.
4  No two activities may start and finish with the same pair of nodes. Otherwise, definition of an activity by a pair of numbers ($i/j$) is ambiguous, and the network is confused.
5  If rule 4 would otherwise be infringed, a dummy activity must be introduced (Figure 17b).
6  A dummy may be used to show a logical dependency where use of only the (real) activity arrows would be insufficient, or would impose unnecessary constraints (Figure 17c).
7  Event numbers should read roughly from left to right. To allow for the insertion of new activities or dummies, the numbers should be multiples of 10, say (like program row numbers in BASIC).

## The Critical Path

There is usually a single path of consecutive activities of minimum total duration, running from start to finish through the project. This is the critical path. It is found by means of a forward pass and a backward pass. Consider five activities at the start of a network, with durations in days as shown in Figure 18a. Event 3 cannot occur before the end of day 5. Event 4 cannot occur before completion of the longest string of activities leading to it. The number in the upper quadrant of node 4 gives the EET, (i.e. the largest number obtained by summing durations along the various routes from event 1 to event 4). This forward pass is carried on from event to event through to the finish, node 39, filling all upper quadrants and giving an overall minimum duration of 73 days (Figure 18b).

This minimum time of completion of the project is now put into the lower quadrant of node 39, and the backward pass made. Event 37 must not occur later than the project duration less the length of the longest string of activities back from node 39 to node 37. The number in the lower quadrant is the smallest number obtained from the various routes back to the node. Carrying this procedure back to node 1 gives an LET in each lower quadrant.

Together the two passes identify a string of activities from start to finish having EET and LET equal. This is the critical path, and any increase of duration of an activity on it will lengthen the

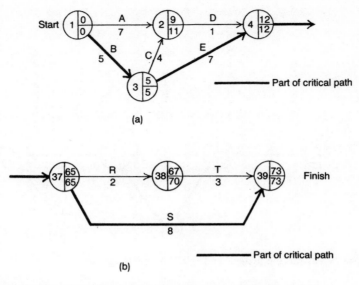

(a)

(b)

*Figure 18* Finding the critical path (a) at the start; (b) at the finish

project. Again, if the overall duration is to be reduced, activities on the critical path must be considered first.

## Float

In Figure 18a, activity C, of duration 4, cannot start before time 5, but need not finish until time 11. It therefore has free float of $(11 - 5 - 4) = 2$ days: delay of C of more than 2 days would delay a succeeding activity. Similarly, in Figure 18b R and T together have a total float of $(73 - 65 - 5) = 3$ days. Delay of more than 3 days in R and T taken together then would delay completion of the project. Critical activities, by definition, have zero float.

The nodes as drawn above are convenient for manual analysis purposes, but it must be remembered that an EET or LET is a number representing a time during the day (here a *day end*): an event is when an activity finishes. The same number also represents the start of the next activity, which is not entirely satisfactory: on the bar chart derived from the network, an activity finishing at day-end $n$ is followed by an activity starting in practice, not at the end of day $n$, but at the beginning of day $(n + 1)$. Thus, to avoid cluttering the diagram with extra numbers, it is necessary to remember that an EET $n$ is an earliest finish (EF) of the preceding activity. The earliest start (ES) of the next is the

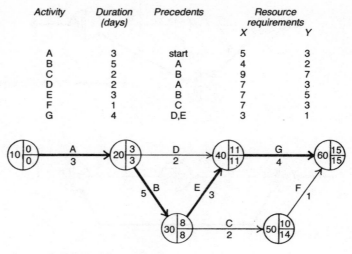

| Activity | Duration (days) | Precedents | Resource requirements X | Y |
|----------|-----------------|------------|-------------------------|---|
| A | 3 | start | 5 | 3 |
| B | 5 | A | 4 | 2 |
| C | 2 | B | 9 | 7 |
| D | 2 | A | 7 | 3 |
| E | 3 | B | 7 | 5 |
| F | 1 | C | 7 | 3 |
| G | 4 | D,E | 3 | 1 |

*Figure 19*   A sample project and initial arrow diagram

beginning of day ($n + 1$). Similarly, an LET $n$ is a latest finish (LF) of the preceding activity; and the latest start (LS) of the next is the beginning of day ($n + 1$). Figure 19 shows the network for a simple seven activity project.

## The Bar Chart

It is not easy to use an arrow diagram as a working document for control purposes. An important deficiency is lack of a time scale; and it is extremely difficult to aggregate resources directly from the diagram (even more so from a precedence diagram). The bar chart, again usually running from right to left, provides both these facilities, together with a display of floats that may be used directly. Logical dependences may be shown with vertical lines, to give a linked bar chart.

The activities may be represented on a bar chart by horizontal bars, of length proportional to activity duration. In the vertical dimension they may have various possible sequences on the diagram: earliest start first, critical first, or according to some other selection criterion. Start and finish times are taken from the network, and linkages should be shown in such a way as to indicate logical dependences and float. It is best to leave a space vertically between activities in a hand-drawn bar chart. Figure 20a shows a bar chart from the network of Figure 19, with the earliest start order of activities.

## Resources

The resources required for each activity may be marked on the bar chart and aggregated day by day, as in Figure 20b. Resources are of several kinds.

1  Non-storable resources (e.g. man-days, plant-hire-days) that are needed daily during an activity. If not used, they cannot be carried over.
2  Storable resources (e.g. cash, materials) that may be saved up if not used or spent.

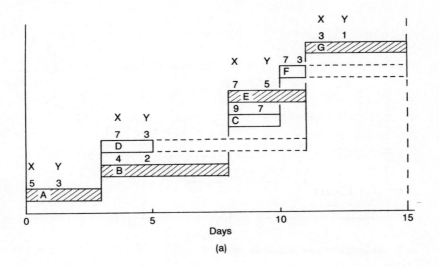

(a)

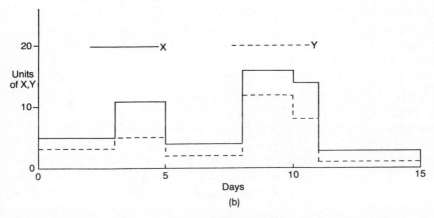

(b)

*Figure 20*   Bar chart and resource profiles from the project of Figure 19

In good project management one aim is to ensure that resource usage is as steady as possible throughout the project. Plant and men are then less likely to stand idle during certain phases. Problems of delivery of materials are likely to be less. By shifting activities, using the bar chart, peaks and troughs may often be smoothed out within the duration of the project as defined by the network. Figure 21a shows one possible improvement on Figure 20a, leading to the resource profile of Figure 21b, which is smoother than the one in Figure 20b. This procedure is known as resource smoothing. If such a smoothing operation gives a profile that is still too lumpy, and requirements cannot be met on some

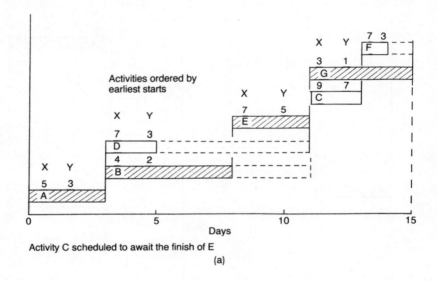

(a)

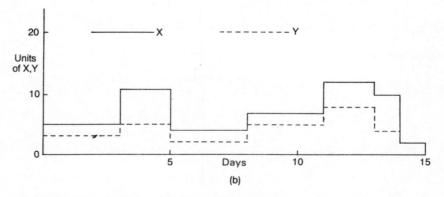

(b)

*Figure 21* Resource smoothing: Figure 20 updated

days, it may be necessary to extend the project duration. This is called resource limiting.

After rescheduling with reference to the bar chart, to allow for resource problems, the changes must be incorporated into the network. This may involve scheduling some activities not to start before a certain day, and some not to finish after a certain day. Following rearrangement of activities on the bar chart, a new network must be drawn, satisfying the original precedence relationships as well as the new schedulings. To ensure that the changes do not impose unnecessary constraints on the network, some additional nodes and/or dummies may have to be used. Figure 22, for example, is a resource smoothed version of Figure 19.

It is found that even the smallest network can lead to substantial complications when resources are considered. Although the basic rules of network analysis are very simple, all projects are different, so that it is impossible to generalise about the details of analysis in all cases. Practice and experience are essential.

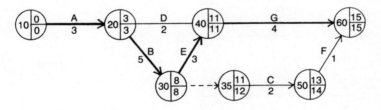

The scheduled start of C de-coupled from the start of E. In this case, no change of critical path, no extension of duration, reduced float of C,F.

*Figure 22*   Network of Figure 19 updated

## 'Crashing' Activities

In some circumstances it may be worth while to reduce the duration of the whole project by reducing the durations of some activities, by extra expenditure on them. Crash costs are incurred. The correct procedure is to look at the activities on the critical path, with a view to reducing the duration of the cheapest activity first. As soon as an activity has been shortened, the whole network must be reconsidered, as the critical path may have changed. If so, the next step is to look at the cheapest activity on the new critical path, rather than at the second cheapest on the original critical

| Activity | Precedents | Normal duration | Minimum duration | Crash cost (£'00/day) |
|---|---|---|---|---|
| A | — | 5 | 3 | 5 |
| B | — | 6 | 5 | 3 |
| C | — | 12 | 10 | 1 |
| D | A | 3 | 2 | 4 |
| E | B,D | 7 | 6 | 2 |

Normal duration of project = 15 days

Step 1  Reduce E to 6 — cost = 2
Step 2  Reduce D to 2 — cost = 4
Step 3  Reduce A to 4 — cost = 5
Step 4  Reduce A to 3
             C to 11 cost  = 9
             B to 5

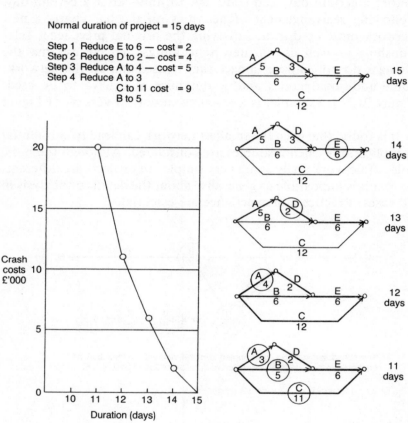

*Figure 23*   'Crash' costs

path. Again, the rules are simple, but will be difficult to apply in the context of a full-scale project. Figure 23 illustrates the principles. A consequence of the application of the above rules is that the curve of crash costs against time saved increases in slope as the duration gets shorter. Whether or not these extra costs can be justified, or off-set by savings in other directions, depends on the particular circumstances of the project.

# The Network as a Contract Document

It was mentioned in Chapter 7 that it is highly desirable to include networks for scheduling in the contract documentation to ensure that both the Owner and the Contractor are quite clear who will bear the extra cost if something goes wrong. Activity durations must be included in the contract if the network is to play a useful part in project control. Care must be taken to use dummies to define contractual sequences of activities. (It might be argued that this section of Chapter 10 should be left until Chapter 11, but it seems reasonable to put it with other discussion of networks.)

A number of interesting examples are given by Lester (1982).

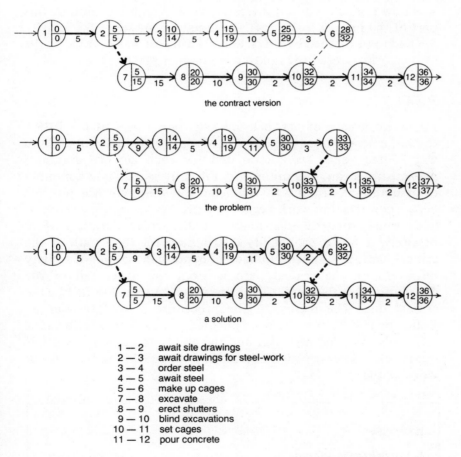

| 1 — 2 | await site drawings |
| 2 — 3 | await drawings for steel-work |
| 3 — 4 | order steel |
| 4 — 5 | await steel |
| 5 — 6 | make up cages |
| 7 — 8 | excavate |
| 8 — 9 | erect shutters |
| 9 — 10 | blind excavations |
| 10 — 11 | set cages |
| 11 — 12 | pour concrete |

*Figure 24* A network in a contract: part of a project for reinforced concrete foundations

One of these will be considered in detail, with reference to Figure 24, showing part of a network agreed for contract purposes. The network is for the Contractor to use, but the site drawings and steel drawings are to be provided by the Owner. According to the contract network, the path 1–2–7–8–9–10–11–12 is critical, giving a duration of 36 days for this part of the project, whilst the path 2–3–4–5–6–10 has float of 4 days. Knowing this, the Owner thought that a delay of 4 days in supplying the drawings for the steelwork would not matter, and the duration of activity 2/3 became 9 days. However, because of this delay, the Contractor found that the order for the steel lost its place in a queue, and activity 4/5 took 11 days, not 10. Path 1–2–3–4–5–6–10–11–12 was now critical, with an increase in the overall duration of this part of the project to 37 days. To maintain the schedule, activity 5/6 had to be crashed by 1 day, and a crash cost was payable by the Owner, who caused the hold-up in the first place.

## PERT

In the early days of network analysis, one aspect of the PERT technique was to treat the duration of the project in a probabilistic way. Three values were estimated for each activity duration: pessimistic, mean, and optimistic. From these data and a number of assumptions of doubtful mathematical validity it was possible before construction work began on a project to deduce a more or less normal probability distribution for the project duration. More precisely, it was a probability distribution for the length of the critical path. It is difficult to handle, because if the sum of activity durations on the critical path is from the lower tail of the distribution for the total, then some other path may in fact be the critical one. The theory of the procedure is well set out by Battersby (1979). It will not be pursued any further here, because full analysis of the network, and the ability to answer 'what if?' questions, is so easy with modern computing facilities that it is not worth while.

### Exercises

1   *Eighteen Men*
Draw the network diagram, bar chart, and resource profile for this project, assuming earliest starts. Reschedule the

activities to limit the number of men required on any day to a maximum of 18. Update the bar chart and network.

| Activity | Duration (days) | Precedents | Men (no.) |
|----------|-----------------|------------|-----------|
| A | 8 | start | 4 |
| B | 7 | start | 8 |
| C | 6 | A | 5 |
| D | 8 | B | 4 |
| E | 4 | B | 8 |
| F | 8 | B | 6 |
| G | 5 | C, D | 5 |
| H | 6 | E | 4 |
| I | 6 | F | 5 |
| J | 10 | G, H, I | 6 |

## 2 Cranes

A building project consists of 12 activities, for 3 of which a crane is needed. Use the information in the table to schedule the project, and to find the shortest overall duration when any number of cranes is available. Reschedule for minimum over-run assuming that only 1 crane will be available.

If liquidated damages will be payable at a rate of £150 per day for over-run, find the amount that could be spent on hiring more than one crane and still break even.

| Activity description | Duration (days) | Resource (cranes) | Precedents |
|----------------------|-----------------|-------------------|------------|
| A | 8 | — | Start |
| B | 5 | — | A |
| C | 6 | — | A |
| D | 8 | 1 | A |
| E | 7 | — | B |
| F | 8 | 1 | C |
| G | 12 | 1 | C |
| H | 6 | — | D, E |
| I | 4 | — | D, E |
| J | 5 | — | F, H |
| K | 4 | — | I |
| L | 4 | — | G, J, K |

## 3 Design

The design of a building is in itself a small project, consisting of the activities listed below. Use the table of costs to find the cheapest way of shortening the project by 1, 2 or 3 weeks.

| Description | Code | Duration (weeks) | Precedents |
|---|---|---|---|
| Preliminary design | A | 2 | Start |
| Specifications | B | 3 | A |
| Site design | C | 2 | A |
| Building design | D | 4 | A |
| Revise spec. for sanction | E | 2 | B |
| Review the project | F | 2 | C, D, E |
| Project out to tender | G | 1 | E, F |

| Code | NORMAL Duration (weeks) | NORMAL Cost £ | CRASH Duration (weeks) | CRASH Cost £ |
|---|---|---|---|---|
| A | 2 | 3000 | 1 | 4000 |
| B | 3 | 2000 | 2 | 2800 |
| C | 2 | 2000 | 1 | 3200 |
| D | 4 | 1500 | 2 | 3000 |
| E | 2 | 1200 | 1 | 1800 |
| F | 2 | 800 | 1 | 1200 |
| G | 1 | 700 | — | — |

D must take either 4 or 2 weeks. *Extra* cost of crashing A is £1000.

## 4   Oxygen

The following data are related to a project for reducing the pollution of a small loch by oxygenation. Draw the arrow diagram and linked bar chart for earliest starts and identify the critical path and normal project duration.

Using the crash cost data, find the extra costs of reducing the duration week by week and draw a graph of extra cost against project duration.

| Description | Code | Duration (weeks) | Precedents |
|---|---|---|---|
| Set up administration | A | 3 | Start |
| Hire personnel | B | 4 | A |
| Obtain materials | C | 4 | A |
| Transport materials | D | 2 | C |
| Train personnel | E | 2 | B |
| Planning | F | 6 | B |
| Set up equipment | G | 3 | D, E |
| Evaluate plan | H | 1 | F |
| Oxygenation | I | 12 | G, H |
| Evaluate effects | J | 2 | I |

| Code | NORMAL Duration (weeks) | Cost £ | CRASH Duration (weeks) | Cost £ |
|------|------|------|------|------|
| A | 3 | 2000 | 2 | 2600 |
| D | 2 | 800 | 1 | 1100 |
| F | 6 | 1000 | 2 | 3000 |
| G | 3 | 1500 | 2 | 2000 |
| I | 12 | 1000 | 11 | 1900 |

F may be reduced a week at a time, at a cost pro rata.

## 5 Plant Installation

Installation of a new machine may be regarded as a small project with 9 activities (A–J). The duration of some of the activities may be reduced by over-time work. For each day that the overall duration is reduced, a bonus of £200 will be paid. Normal and crash costs are as shown in the table, but the reduction available in any activity duration is to be all or nothing. The costs of non-crashed activities are unaltered.

| Code | Description | Precedents | NORMAL Duration (days) | Cost £ | CRASH Duration (days) | Cost £ |
|------|------|------|------|------|------|------|
| A | clear site | start | 2 | — | — | — |
| B | excavate | A | 2 | 400 | 1 | 500 |
| C | founds | B | 2 | 1100 | 1 | 1250 |
| D | cure | C | 7 | — | — | — |
| E | order machine | start | 1 | — | — | — |
| F | deliver machine | E | 11 | — | — | — |
| G | instal machine | D, F | 4 | 480 | 3 | 600 |
| H | power supply | A | 16 | 500 | 12 | 600 |
| J | test machine | G, H | 2 | — | — | — |

(a) Construct the arrow diagram and bar chart for the normal project and find the normal finishing day.

(b) By crashing some activities, in order of decreasing value for money, find the schedule financially optimum for the contractor.

(c) Having just started on the optimum schedule, the Contractor finds that delivery of the machine will be delayed by one extra day. What should the Contractor do?

(d) Boulders are found when the excavation is started, so that B will take an extra 3 days. What effect does this have on the value of the project to the Contractor?

## 6  Weekly Costs

Part of a capital project is to be completed by the activities listed in the table, which gives the precedents for each activity, its duration in weeks, and its weekly cost.

(a)  Construct an arrow diagram to show earliest and latest start times and the critical path. Ensure that there are no unnecessary logical constraints.

(b)  Construct the corresponding bar chart, ordered by earliest starts.

(c)  Find the resource profile for weekly cost.

(d)  Show on the bar chart how the activities may be rescheduled so that the total cost in any week does not exceed £5000.

(e)  Revise the profile of (c).

(f)  Revise the network to accommodate the new schedule.

| Activity | Precedents | Duration (weeks) | Cost per week £'000 |
|----------|------------|------------------|---------------------|
| A | Start | 3 | 2 |
| B | A | 9 | 3 |
| C | B | 3 | 3 |
| D | C, J, K | 3 | 2 |
| E | Start | 1 | 3 |
| F | E | 1 | 2 |
| G | Start | 3 | 2 |
| H | A, F | 3 | 1 |
| J | H | 2 | 1 |
| K | B, H | 1 | 1 |
| L | K | 2 | 2 |

## 7  Ten Men

The activities of a small project may be represented by the network shown in the diagram. Activity durations and the number of men required for each one are given in the table. In fact only 10 men are available, so that the schedule must be rearranged from the simple one of earliest starts.

Show on a bar chart how the activities must be scheduled to meet the resource constraint, and revise the network appropriately.

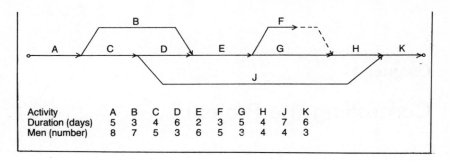

| Activity | A | B | C | D | E | F | G | H | J | K |
|---|---|---|---|---|---|---|---|---|---|---|
| Duration (days) | 5 | 3 | 4 | 6 | 2 | 3 | 5 | 4 | 7 | 6 |
| Men (number) | 8 | 7 | 5 | 3 | 6 | 5 | 3 | 4 | 4 | 3 |

## Appendix

### *Arrow and precedence diagrams*

(a) An arrow diagram gives an impression of the passage of time, even though unscaled, that is difficult to achieve with a precedence diagram, especially if the latter is drawn on a standard pre-printed sheet of nodes.

(b) Arrow diagram data may be entered into a computing package, and updated from time to time, more easily and quickly than a precedence diagram.

(c) The arrows provide plenty of room for activity data, which is helpful when updating from the barchart, and indicate the flow of the project.

(d) Each node on an arrow diagram belongs to at least two activities so that data written at the node require careful interpretation. On a precedence diagram, data at a node belong to only one activity.

(e) With an arrow diagram, the logic of the activities can in general be shown fully only with the use of dummies. No dummies are needed with a precedence diagram although they can sometimes be introduced to clarify a precedence diagram.

(f) With a precedence diagram it is easy to use the link lines to show different periods of overlap of the activities. This can only be done in an arrow diagram by subdividing activities so that part of one runs in parallel with part of another.

# Chapter 11

# Controlling the Project

Unless the Owner is also the main Contractor, the burden of control of the project falls to the Contractor, particularly when the contract is of the lump sum type. A large amount of evidence has been gathered together by Kharbanda *et al* (1980) suggesting that this is the most difficult aspect of a large project. In addition to ensuring that materials are not lost or wasted, the Contractor aims at efficient use of labour and plant, with both working at their proper rates, and with a minimum of idle time. Efficient use of sub-contractors must be included, as it is expensive, for example, to have a sub-contractor held up beyond the scheduled starting date because prior work is not complete. Control effort may at times appear to be directed separately at time and costs, but they are of course closely related.

The essence of control is to compare, at frequent intervals, what has actually happened with what was earlier planned to happen. There may be good reason for the variance (in the accountant's sense). Otherwise, corrective action is required to reduce the discrepancy. The estimates and the schedules of the project activities were drawn up on the basis of the best information available at the time, which was almost certainly less complete and accurate than would have been wished. Nevertheless, a plan is necessary before work starts. As work proceeds and information is collected, actual achievement may be compared with the plan. Any deviation calls for scrutiny: either the original plan was unrealistic in some way, or corrective action is required to put the project back on course.

To keep a running check on costs of materials is difficult for a number of reasons. There are time lags between materials being ordered, received, invoiced, used and paid for. Procedures will differ from one contractor, and from one supplier, to another, and are matters of professional accountancy. There is the necessary slowness of the procedures if the paper work is to be handled accurately, as required for accounting reasons. There is the question of when the ordered material was actually used. Figure 25 illustrates in a simple way the problem of control in relation to the S-curve discussed in Chapter 8. After the work is completed, the Contractor would find, with hindsight, that three S-curves have been plotted: one for the value of work done, as certified by the Engineer; one for his own expenses; and one for the cash received from the Owner. The difference between expenses and receipts represents working capital at any time, which is another way of looking at the cash flows of Chapter 8. The important question is: can the Contractor plot these curves month by month, say, as the project proceeds (see Figure 25)? In general, the answer is only roughly, and not fast enough. Nevertheless, much effort by a firm's management information systems is put into attempts to solve the problem. It is discussed in some detail by Kharbanda *et al.* (1980).

The Contractor is much concerned to find useful, quick and effective short cuts to obtaining information that can be used effectively for control purposes. This chapter is mainly concerned with some of these techniques.

The first is based on Chapter 19 in Lester (1982), and concerns

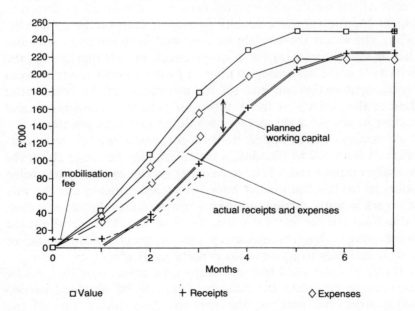

*Figure 25* The Contractor's project control curves: effect of time lags; cash received in advance, if any, is a mobilisation fee

value hours, where a "flash photograph" of sub-divisions of an activity is taken on a routine basis, preferably at least once a week. Analysis of the project into activities for scheduling by means of the bar chart leads to units that are generally too large for control purposes. They must be broken down into what will be called sub-activities that are small enough for an inspector to be able to decide, in a matter of minutes, say, what percentage of completeness each sub-activity has reached. As with the activities themselves, it is important not to have so small a sub-division that the control system becomes excessively complex.

For controlling a project, advantage should be taken of any facilities that already exist for some other purpose. For example, the amount of work that has been done on a sub-activity may conveniently be found from labour records. An administrative system already exists, as time cards have to be completed, and processed for wages purposes. Further, experience has shown that the number of man-hours worked on a sub-activity (actual hours) is a useful measure of effort put into it so far. The actual hours may or may not correspond to a satisfactory percentage complete.

In drawing up a schedule of sub-activities, a number of man-hours, called budget hours, are allocated to each one. The status of the whole activity may now be represented as shown in Figure 26, and various calculations may be done on the data in the table. The values there might be described as rough and ready, but they meet the need (a) for a quick check on whether or not the activity is going according to plan, (b) for a pointer towards areas requiring investigation and (c) for a forecast of the completion date of the activity. A large difference between actual hours and budget hours for a sub-activity would be one such pointer.

Assuming that the budget hours as planned give a fair representation of the work to be done, a statement may be made about the overall completeness of the activity, from the ratio of total value hours so far to total budget hours. A mean efficiency for the way the work is being carried out may be expressed as the ratio of total value hours so far to total actual hours so far. This has the slight disadvantage that the efficiency can be greater than unity, or 100%, contrary to more usual definitions of efficiency.

It is useful to have a forecast of the total man-hours that will be required to complete the activity. This can be obtained in two ways: from the sum of the forecast final hours for all the sub-activities individually; and from the total budget hours and the efficiency. A large difference between these is itself a useful

An activity has been divided for control purposes into sub-activities
A to N
Value hours so far     $(5) = (2)*(4)/100$
Forecast final hours   $(6) = (3)*100/(4)$

| Sub-act. | Budget hours | Actual hours | % comp. | Value hours | Forecast final hrs |
|---|---|---|---|---|---|
| (1) | (2) | (3) | (4) | (5) | (6) |
| A | 500 | 430 | 100 | 500 | 430 |
| B | 120 | 130 | 100 | 120 | 130 |
| C | 400 | 270 | 40 | 160 | 675 |
| D | 450 | 250 | 70 | 315 | 357 |
| E | 200 | 150 | 90 | 180 | 167 |
| F | 80 | 20 | 10 | 8 | 200 |
| G | 400 | 30 | 10 | 40 | 300 |
| H | 300 | 20 | 5 | 15 | 400 |
| I | 150 | 20 | 15 | 23 | 133 |
| J | 70 | 0 | 0 | 0 | 70 |
| K | 50 | 10 | 5 | 3 | 200 |
| L | 100 | 0 | 0 | 0 | 100 |
| M | 200 | 0 | 0 | 0 | 200 |
| N | 500 | 0 | 0 | 0 | 500 |
| (1) | (2) | (3) | (4) | (5) | (6) |

Total final hours—forecast 1
[Sum of column (6)]                              = 3862 hours

Total final hours—forecast 2
[Sum of (2)] * [sum of (3)]/[sum of (5)] = 3435 hours

Overall % complete
[sum of (5)] * 100/[sum of (2)]            = 39%

Efficiency
[sum of (5)] * 100/[sum of (3)]            = 102%

*Figure 26*  Status of an activity: value hours

indication that something needs investigation. It should be noted
that a convention of terms is being used, in that 'total' refers to a
summation over sub-activities, whereas 'final' means cumulatively
in time.

A simple example of a discrepancy between the forecasts is
shown in Figure 27. An activity is divided into three sub-activities
A, B and C. In Figure 27a all are going according to plan, but in
Figure 27b there is a large difference between the actual hours and

(a)   Three sub-activities all going well

| Sub-act. | Budget hours | Actual hours | % comp. | Value hours | Forecast final hrs |
|---|---|---|---|---|---|
| (1) | (2) | (3) | (4) | (5) | (6) |
| A | 910 | 346 | 40 | 364 | 865 |
| B | 570 | 212 | 35 | 200 | 606 |
| C | 390 | 283 | 70 | 273 | 404 |

Total final hours—forecast 1
[sum of (6)]                                                   = 1875

Total final hours—forecast 2
[sum of (2)] * [sum of (3)]/[sum of (5)]     = 1880

(b)   Sub-activity B seriously held up

| Sub-act. | Budget hours | Actual hours | % comp. | Value hours | Forecast final hrs |
|---|---|---|---|---|---|
| (1) | (2) | (3) | (4) | (5) | (6) |
| A | 910 | 346 | 40 | 364 | 865 |
| B | 570 | 406 | 15 | 86 | 2707 |
| C | 390 | 283 | 70 | 273 | 404 |

Total final hours—forecast 1
[sum(6)]                                                        = 3976

Total final hours—forecast 2
[sum(2)] * [sum(3)]/[sum(5)]                       = 2679

(c)   Some time on sub-activity B written off

| Sub-act. | Budget hours | Actual hours | % comp. | Value hours | Forecast final hrs |
|---|---|---|---|---|---|
| (1) | (2) | (3) | (4) | (5) | (6) |
| A | 910 | 346 | 40 | 364 | 865 |
| B1 | 570 | 86 | 15 | 86 | 573 |
| B2 | 0 | 320 | 100 | 0 | 320 |
| C | 390 | 283 | 70 | 273 | 404 |

Total final hours—forecast 1
[sum(6)]                                                        = 2163

Total final hours—forecast 2
[sum-(2)] * [sum(3) − 320]/[sum(5)] + 320     = 2171

*Figure 27*   A sub-activity held up

value hours for B. Clearly B calls for investigation. There is also a substantial difference between the two forecasts of total final hours. The matter may be resolved by further sub-dividing B, into a part $B_1$, for which the actual hours worked is put equal to the value hours spent so far on B as a whole; and a part $B_2$, for which there were no budgeted hours, taking up the balance of actual hours. In effect, a fraction of the actual hours has been written off. The two forecasts of total hours are now more nearly equal (Figure 27c).

In the early stages of the activity, these forecasts are likely to be wildly inaccurate. However, as information accumulates, data from the analysis may be plotted as shown in Figures 28 and 29. Plotting total forecast hours and total actual hours at intervals of one month, say, the curves may be extrapolated until they meet. The meeting point indicates the completion date, as the two quantities must then be equal. Alternatively, the curve of total value hours against time will, by definition, meet the total budget hours line at completion.

Towards the completion date, the extrapolations and the two forecasts of the completion date of the whole activity become more accurate. The two cases of Figures 28 and 29 illustrate the point. As no activity can have two completion dates, the mean of the two forecasts may be used for planning purposes.

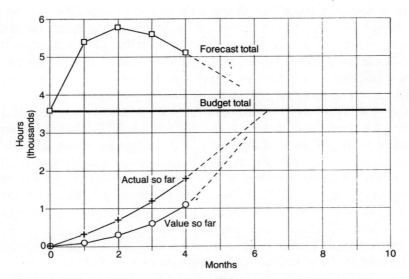

*Figure 28*  Forecasting an activity completion date: extrapolation to completion date 1

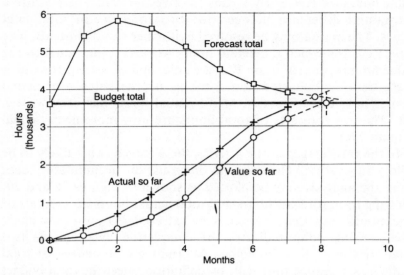

*Figure 29*   Forecasting an activity completion date: extrapolation to completion date 2

Another technique for project control, that might also be classed as coarse accountancy, is concerned with monetary inflation. The duration of a large construction project, say, is likely to extend over a period of significant inflation. As costs exceed the amounts allowed for in the estimate, the important question arises: how much of the excess can be attributed to inflation, and how much to wastage of one kind or another? The category of wastage may include labour standing idle (man-hours that have to be paid for, in addition to those actually incurred in doing the job); theft of materials; hired plant standing idle (loss of machine-hours, as with loss of man-hours); or jobs genuinely taking longer than had been anticipated. It is clear from this list that there are many items of expenditure subject to price increases and the contract should allow for bona fide price inflation. How can the Contractor check whether or not there is a wastage element in the costs that is outside the terms of the contract? How can the Contractor divide the difference between allowed costs and actual costs into an inflation element and a wastage element?

Monetary inflation is an extraordinarily difficult phenomenon to quantify. Price indexes are commonly quoted and used, despite their doubtful meaning in particular cases (see Kendall (1969)). They have, however, the advantage of giving at least a rough and ready indication of what is happening, and it has been generally agreed that price adjustments between the Contractor and the Owner may be based on them. In principle, it can be envisaged that the vast number of items of a project, from the very small to the very large, could each be investigated for inflation. Such a

| 2/1 | Demolitions | 2/24 | Softwood joinery |
|---|---|---|---|
| 2/2 | Site preparation, excavation and disposal | 2/25 | Hardwood joinery |
| | | 2/26 | Ironmongery |
| 2/3 | Hardcore and imported filling | 2/27 | Steelwork |
| | | 2/28 | Steel windows and doors |
| 2/4 | General piling | | |
| 2/5 | Steel sheet piling | 2/29 | Aluminium windows and doors |
| 2/6 | Concrete | | |
| 2/7 | Reinforcement | 2/30 | Miscellaneous metalwork |
| 2/8 | Structural precast and prestressed concrete units | 2/31 | Cast iron pipes and fittings |
| | | 2/32 | Plastic pipes and fittings |
| 2/9 | Non-structural precast concrete components | 2/33 | Copper tubes, fittings and cylinders |
| 2/10 | Formwork | 2/34 | Mild steel pipes, fittings and tanks |
| 2/11 | Brickwork and blockwork | | |
| 2/12 | Natural stone | 2/35 | Boilers, pumps and radiators |
| 2/13 | Asphalt work | | |
| 2/14 | Slate and tile roofing | 2/36 | Sanitary fittings |
| 2/15 | Asbestos cement sheet roofing and cladding | 2/37 | Insulation |
| | | 2/38 | Plastering (all types) to walls and ceilings |
| 2/16 | Plastic coated steel sheet roofing and cladding | | |
| 2/17 | Aluminium sheet roofing and cladding | 2/39 | Beds and screeds (all types) to floors, roofs and pavings |
| 2/18 | Built-up felt roofing | 2/40 | Dry partitions and linings |
| 2/19 | Built-up felt roofing on metal decking | 2/41 | Tiling and terrazzo work |
| | | 2/42 | Suspended ceilings (dry construction) |
| 2/20 | Carpentry, manufactured boards and softwood flooring | | |
| | | 2/43 | Glass, mirrors and patent glazing |
| 2/21 | Hardwood flooring | 2/44 | Decorations |
| 2/22 | Tile and sheet flooring (vinyl, thermoplastic, linoleum and other synthetic materials) | 2/45 | Drainage pipework (other than cast iron) |
| | | 2/46 | Fencing, gates and screens |
| | | 2/47 | Bituminous surfacing to roads and paths |
| 2/23 | Jointless flooring (epoxy resin type) | 2/48 | Soft landscaping |

*Figure 30* Work types (categories) for indexing in building contracts (reproduced by kind permission of the Controller of Her Majesty's Stationery Office; taken from *Price adjustments formulae for building contracts*, published by HMSO)

procedure, if attempted, would be impossibly protracted, that is to say, too slow for control purposes. A more practical approach is to analyse each activity into work types, or categories, as discussed in Chapter 4, on estimation. Aggregating the allowed cost for each work type in all activities gives a figure to which a price index may be applied. The procedure is of very great complexity, and its effectiveness depends on appropriate price index values being not only available, but up-to-date enough to be useful for project control purposes. A good idea of what is involved is given in the document 'Price Adjustment Formulae for Building Contracts' (HMSO 1977), which also recommends procedures and forms for completion, rather in the manner of conditions of contract. Figure 30 shows a list of work categories on which price adjustments may be based.

A price index is related to a base date. In general the base date of an index is not the date of tender for the contract, which is usually the date on which the project is deemed to have started. Suppose that a work category W was indexed at $I_t$ at the start; and is now indexed at $I_p$. The actual cost of this work category over the whole, or part, of the project up to the present has been $A$. In relation to the original estimate, the cost of W up to the present (i.e. the allowed cost) should have been $B$. The variance $(A - B)$ may be considered as the sum of two parts: $Y$, due to wastage; and $Z$, due to inflation:

$$A - B = Y + Z$$

Now the present indexed value of $B$ is $B \times \dfrac{I_p}{I_t}$

so that            $Z = B \times (I_p/I_t - 1)$
and therefore    $Y = A - B - Z$
                        $= A - B \times (I_p/I_t)$

Knowing $A$ and $B$ from internal accounting, and finding $I_p$ and $I_t$ from published tables, the wastage element $Y$ can be found for the work category W so far. A similar procedure will yield a wastage element for other work categories. An example will show how this works. For simplicity, problems arising from time lags (e.g. in receipt of invoices, or collection of other data) will be ignored.

Consider three activities of the project, that will, when finished, have required certain (different) numbers of units of work category W. The cost of each unit of W (the unit rate) in the different activities is made up of labour, materials, plant and sub-contractor costs. This information is derived from the original estimates (Figure 31a). From last month end to this month end, the status of these activities has changed, as shown in Figure 31b, from which the allowed costs of work category W for this month may be found for each activity, and in total (i.e. £6280). This total is $B$.

It has been found from invoices for this month that the actual

---

(a) *Calculation of unit rates for work category W*

Data from tender documents (at that time $l_t = 124$)

| Activity | Costs per unit of W (£) | | | | Unit rate £ | Total units to complete the activity |
|---|---|---|---|---|---|---|
| | Lab. | Mat. | Pla. | S/con | | |
| A | 23 | 35 | 38 | 0 | 96 | 57 |
| B | 46 | 21 | 0 | 0 | 67 | 32 |
| C | 22 | 15 | 0 | 52 | 89 | 18 |

(b) *Allowed cost for this month*

Status at this month end (now $l_p = 153$)

| Activity | Unit rate £ | Units completed | | Allowed cost for this month £ |
|---|---|---|---|---|
| | | Last m/end | This m/end | |
| A | 96 | 13 | 48 | $(48 - 13) \times 96 = 3360$ |
| B | 67 | 6 | 27 | $(27 - 6) \times 67 = 1407$ |
| C | 89 | 0 | 17 | $(17 - 0) \times 89 = 1513$ |

$$B = £6280$$

The allowed cost for work category W for this month, for all activities, corrected for inflation is given by

$$B \times (l_p/l_t)$$
$$= 6280 \times (153/124)$$
$$= £7749$$

(NB The indexes apply to work category W in all activities.)

(c) *Status of work category W this month*

From invoices for this month related to work category W: $A = £9824$
Therefore, wastage this month on W is given by

$$A - B \times (l_p/l_t)$$
$$= 9824 - 7749$$
$$= £2075$$

*Figure 31* Inflation and wastage

cost of W for these activities (i.e. $A$) is £9824. Since the tender date, the index for W has risen from 124 to 153. The wastage of W on these activities for this month is therefore (Figure 31c) $Y = 9824 - 6280 \times (153/124) = £2075$.

This figure indicates wastage in work category W, but does not show in which of the activities it occurred. Further detailed investigation would be needed to establish the source of the wastage closely enough for effective action. None of the procedures mentioned in this chapter is likely to point out immediately and precisely where corrective action should be taken. What they do is to show when something is going wrong somewhere, and making it worth while to take a closer look. To look closely, everywhere, all the time, would be too expensive.

## Exercises

### 1 Half-way status

A substantial part of a project consists of ten sub-activities A–J. The following data show the status of this part when it is roughly half complete. From the data, make and compare two forecasts of the total final hours that will be required for completion. Estimate the overall percentage complete and comment on the efficiency with which the work is being carried out.

| 1 | 2 Budget hours | 3 Actual hours | 4 % complete | 5 Value hours | 6 Forecast final hours |
|---|---|---|---|---|---|
| A | 260 | 285 | 100 | | |
| B | 450 | 440 | 100 | | |
| C | 380 | 395 | 100 | | |
| D | 410 | 255 | 70 | | |
| E | 570 | 305 | 50 | | |
| F | 420 | 315 | 80 | | |
| G | 290 | 205 | 50 | | |
| H | 330 | 125 | 30 | | |
| I | 340 | 70 | 20 | | |
| J | 190 | 0 | 0 | | |

### 2 A delayed sub-activity

Within the table below, of data for the sub-activities A, B, C, D, a large discrepancy will be found between the actual hours and value hours for C at a stage when substantially less than one half of the whole activity is complete. By sub-dividing C into two parts $C_1$ and $C_2$, find a more realistic forecast of the total final hours than can be obtained directly from the first version of the table.

| 1 | 2<br>Budget<br>hours | 3<br>Actual<br>hours | 4<br>%<br>complete | 5<br>Value<br>hours | 6<br>Forecast<br>final hours |
|---|---|---|---|---|---|
| A | 863 | 185 | 20 | 173 | 925 |
| B | 235 | 127 | 60 | 141 | 212 |
| C | 712 | 594 | 30 | 214 | 1980 |
| D | 486 | 87 | 20 | 97 | 435 |
| | 2296 | 993 | | 625 | 3552 |

## 3 Forecasting completion

The following data, in units of 1000 man-hours, concern a project for which the budget total man-hours was 9200. Values for the total actual hours so far, the total value hours so far, and the forecast total actual hours were calculated each week.

Find by graphical methods the forecast, as it would have been at the week ends 5, 10 and 15.

| Week<br>end | Total<br>actual hours | Total<br>value hours | Forecast<br>total<br>actual hours |
|---|---|---|---|
| 1 | 0.5 | 0.2 | 12.5 |
| 2 | 0.7 | 0.5 | 13.4 |
| 3 | 1.4 | 0.6 | 14.9 |
| 4 | 1.5 | 0.9 | 15.3 |
| 5 | 2.0 | 1.0 | 14.8 |
| 6 | 2.3 | 1.3 | 14.9 |
| 7 | 2.9 | 1.5 | 15.1 |
| 8 | 3.6 | 1.7 | 14.6 |
| 9 | 4.0 | 2.2 | 14.7 |
| 10 | 4.9 | 2.4 | 14.1 |
| 11 | 5.8 | 3.1 | 14.1 |
| 12 | 7.4 | 3.3 | 14.3 |
| 13 | 8.5 | 4.0 | 13.2 |
| 14 | 9.3 | 4.4 | 13.3 |
| 15 | 9.7 | 5.4 | 12.6 |
| 16 | 10.3 | 5.9 | 12.0 |
| 17 | 11.1 | 6.9 | 12.0 |

## 4   Inflation

Use the following data to evaluate the wastage in month 14 in work category W (summed over all the activities in which it occurs).

(a)   *Calculation of unit rates for work category W*
          *(at the time of tender, when $I_t = 117$)*

| Activity | Costs per unit of W | | | £ | Unit rate | Total units to complete |
| :---: | :---: | :---: | :---: | :---: | :---: | :---: |
| | Lab. | Mat. | Pla. | S/con. | £ | the activity |
| A | 12 | 48 | 0 | 77 | | 95 |
| B | 21 | 55 | 83 | 0 | | 102 |
| C | 54 | 19 | 68 | 52 | | 73 |
| D | 8 | 0 | 0 | 105 | | 34 |
| E | 37 | 49 | 30 | 0 | | 62 |

(b)   *Allowed cost B in month 14*
Status at month end 14 (now $I_p = 161$)

| Activity | Unit rate £ | Units completed by m/end 13 | Units completed by m/end 14 | Allowed cost for month 14 £ |
| :---: | :---: | :---: | :---: | :---: |
| A | | 87 | 95 | = |
| B | | 70 | 81 | = |
| C | | 33 | 42 | = |
| D | | 0 | 15 | = |
| E | | 0 | 8 | = |
| | | | | $B =$ |

The allowed cost for work category W for month 14, for all activities, corrected for inflation is:

(c)   *Status of work category W at month end 14*

From invoices received related to work
category W in month 14:                    $A = £9873$
Therefore, wastage in month 14 on W is:

# Part IV
# Owner and Main Contractor

# Chapter 12

# Completion and Hand-Over

In the Introduction it was stated that it is characteristic of a capital project that it has a start and a finish. The reader may therefore have been surprised to read in Chapter 2 that often the starting point is not easy to identify. It may be taken as the date of sanction, the date of submission of a tender, or as the date of award of the contract, depending on the point at issue, and between which parties. It is difficult also to choose a single date as marking the finish of the project, although much time may have been spent in trying to forecast it. In spite of this problem, something must be said about the way in which the project is brought to a close, bearing in mind that the capital project may in fact be only part of the Owner's project.

This chapter can be regarded as a continuation of Chapters 6 and 7, as it is much concerned with the Contractor carrying out the contractual tasks. Unless conditions of physical impossibility arise, or major defects are discovered in the design, the Contractor is under a legal obligation to complete the works. In the contract the Contractor has claimed to be able to do what the Owner has asked for, and it was the Contractor's responsibility to check that this was true. Therefore, the Contractor must do whatever is necessary, whether or not it is described in the contract documents, including 'indispensibly necessary work'; and 'contingently necessary work', due to unforeseen difficulties. The latter may not necessarily be claimed for in a lump sum contract, as the Owner does not warrant that the project is feasible.

If the work can be done before the completion date in the contract (and at the agreed price, for a lump sum contract), all is well. On the other hand, delays are a source of complications. For a full discussion of the legal aspects of the situation, the reader is referred to Wallace (1978). All that is attempted here is to mention some of the main points that arise.

The Engineer certifies from time to time that parts of the work are complete, to his satisfaction. In due course, the Engineer must certify that the whole is complete. Regarding the completion date in the contract, the Engineer may, if there is good reason, grant an extension of time. An over-run without good reason may render the Contractor liable to pay the Owner liquidated damages. In the contract, the Owner gives an estimate of the extra costs per day that he will incur for any over-run of completion date, and these costs are the basis for the liquidated damages. They are not to be regarded as a penalty. For example, if the Engineer should see fit to grant an extension after liquidated damages have been paid, the Contractor may recover them from the Owner.

The contract makes provision for part of the value of certificated work to be retained by the Owner for the time being (retentions). Payment of an instalment of the retentions is an indication to the Contractor that he will no longer be liable for liquidated damages. It also has the effect of indicating the commencement of a Maintenance Period, or Period of Defects Liability.

So that payments to the Contractor may not be held up unduly, the Engineer may issue a Certificate of Substantial Completion of part, or indeed of the whole, of the works, and the maintenance period runs from that time. Following the maintenance period, and all necessary actions having been taken by the Contractor to the satisfaction of the Engineer, the latter issues a Certificate of Maintenance. There may be other matters, taking more time, to be resolved before the Final Certificate is issued.

After completion, or substantial completion, of part of the works, it may be occupied or used by the Owner, but if this option is taken the period of maintenance is deemed to be over.

The above comments are generally applicable to capital projects. If the project in its entirety is to set up a manufacturing plant there are additional matters for the attention of the Engineer (see, for example, IChemE 1981). To enable the Owner to take charge of the plant systematically, the contract should include a Schedule of Take-Over Procedures. If the Engineer calls for procedures that are not in the contract, they must be regarded as variations, and as such paid for by the Owner. After satisfactory completion of the take-over procedures the Engineer issues a Take-Over Certificate. The Owner then carries out performance tests according to a Schedule of Performance Tests, of which the results are evaluated jointly by the Owner or Engineer and the Contractor. Provided the plant operates correctly at the designed rates of feed, production, and consumption of utilities, and makes an acceptable product, the Engineer issues an Acceptance Certificate.

Liability for maintenance rests with the Contractor for the period ending one year after issue of the Take-Over Certificate. At the end of that time, and provided the Contractor has carried out any necessary replacements or repairs to the satisfaction of the Engineer, the latter may issue a Final Certificate. Replacements or repairs may require repetition of some take-over procedures or performance tests, which must be properly certificated, and may lead to extension of the maintenance period before final certification.

## Exercises

1   Study the model conditions of the contracts drawn up by the engineering institutions and allocate the responsibilities for actions following completion of a capital project to the various dramatis personae.

2   What are the implications for future action of completion of, say, a civil engineering project as compared with completion of a manufacturing facility?

# Bibliography

ALLEN, D. H. (1985) *Economic Evaluation of Projects*. Institution of Chemical Engineers.

BAASEL, W. D. (1977) *Preliminary Chemical Engineering and Plant Design*. Elsevier.

BAIER, M. (1985) *Elements of Direct Marketing*. McGraw-Hill.

BAINES, A. *et al*. (1969) *Research in the Chemical Industry*. Elsevier.

BATTERSBY, A. (1979) *Network Analysis*. Macmillan.

BROMWICH, M. (1976) *The Economics of Capital Budgeting*. Penguin.

BSI (1987) *British Standard No. 4335. Glossary of terms used in project network techniques*.

BSI (1981–1984) *British Standard No. 6046 Pts. 1–4. Use of network techniques in project management*.

CLARK, F. D. and LORENZONI, F. B. (1985) *Applied Cost Engineering*. Marcel Dekker.

COOKE, B. (1981) *Contract Planning and Contractual Procedure*. Macmillan.

CROWSON, P. C. F. and RICHARDS, B. A. (1975) *Economics for Managers*. Arnold.

DE LA MARE, R. F. (1982) *Manufacturing Systems Economics*. Holt Rinehart & Winston.

EILON, S. (1984) *The Art of Reckoning*. Academic Press.

GUTHRIE, K. M. (1969) *Chemical Engineering*. March:114.

HACKNEY, J. W. (1965) *Control and Management of Capital Projects*. Wiley.

HARRIS, F. and McCAFFER, R. (1983) *Modern Construction Management*. Granada.

HARRISON, F. L. (1981) *Advanced Project Management*. Gower.

HMSO (1977) *Price Adjustment Formulae for Building Contracts*.

ICE (1973) *Conditions of Contract*. 5th edn. Insitution of Civil Engineers.

ICE (1985) *Civil Engineering Standard Method of Measurement*. Institution of Civil Engineers.

IChemE (1976) *Conditions of Contract for Process Plants: Reimbursable Contracts in the UK*. Institution of Chemical Engineers.

IChemE (1981) *Conditions of Contract for Process Plants: Lump Sum Contracts in the UK*. Institution of Chemical Engineers.

IChemE (1982) *Capital Cost Estimating*. Institution of Chemical Engineers & Association of Cost Engineers.

IMechE (1982) *General Conditions of Contract-Home Contracts with Erection*. Institution of Mechanical Engineers, Institution of Electrical Engineers & Association of Consulting Engineers.

Kendall, M. G. (1969) The Early History of Index Numbers. *Review of the International Statistical Institute*. **37**:1.

Kharbanda, O. P. *et al.* (1980) *Project Cost Control*. Pitman.

Lang, H. J. (1948) Simplified Approach to Preliminary Cost Estimates. *Chemical Engineering*. June:112.

Lester, A. (1982) *Project Planning and Control*. Butterworths.

Lock, D. (1984) *Project Management*. Gower.

Miller, C. A. (1965) Factor Estimates Refined for Appropriation of Funds. *American Association of Cost Engineers Bulletin*. **7**:92.

Mishan, E. J. (1972) *Elements of Cost-Benefit Analysis*. Allen & Unwin.

Perry, J. G. and Thompson, P. A. (1978) *Target and Cost-reimbursable Construction Contracts*. CIRIA Report.

Peters, G. (1981) *Project Management and Construction Control*. Construction Press.

Snowdon, M. (1977) *Management of Engineering Projects*. Butterworths.

Sugden, R. (1987) *The Principles of Practical Cost-Benefit Analysis*. Oxford University Press.

Thompson, P. A. (1981) *Organisation and Economics of Construction*. McGraw-Hill.

Twiss, B. (1986) *Managing Technological Innovation*. Longman.

Wallace, I. N. D. (1976) *Hudson's Building and Engineering Contracts*. 10th edn. Sweet & Maxwell.

Wallace, I. N. D. (1978) *The ICE Conditions of Contract: A Commentary*. 5th edn. Sweet & Maxwell.

Wearne, S. H. (ed.) (1974) *Control of Engineering Projects*. Arnold.

Woodward, J. F. (1975) *Construction Management and Design*. Macmillan.

# Index

Acceptance Certificate, 107
accountancy, external, 15
accountancy, internal, 15
activities, 73, 92
activity network, 50
activity on node, 73
actual cost, 96, 98
actual hours, 92
actual hours written off, 95
admeasurement, 23, 46, 50
allowed cost, 47, 96, 98
Architect, the, 13
arrow diagram, 73, 89
award (of contract), 14, 36

backward pass, 76
ball park costings, 9
bar chart, 50, 73, 78
bar chart, linked, 78
battery limits area, 24
bill of quantities, 21, 35, 50
bonus (to contractor), 44, 46
budget estimate, 10
budget estimate, cost of, 19
budget hours, 92

calendar, 73
carbon steel, 25, 26
cash flows, 55, 57
categories of projects, 4
Certificate of Maintenance, 106
Certificate of Substantial
    Completion, 106
certification, 14, 58
CESMM, 23
check lists, 12, 33
chemical engineering, 5
claims, 36, 41
classification of projects, 41
clearance (of site), 51
client, 3
coarse accountancy, 96
commissioning, 6
communication, 51

completion, 18, 106
completion date, 92, 105
conditions of tender, 34
construction, 5
contingency allowance, 18
contingently necessary work, 105
contract, 48
contribution, 14, 60, 65, 66
control (of cost), 18
control (of project), 90
copyright, 51
cost estimating, 9
cost plus contract, 42, 44
cost-benefit analysis, 9
CPA, 73
crash costs, 81
critical path, 76
critical path method, 73

Defects Liability, Period of, 106
definition, 13
delays, 105
departmentalised project, 5
design, 18
design and build, 5
discounting, 56, 61
dummy activity, 76, 81

earliest event time, 75
earliest finish, 77
earliest start, 77
efficiency, 92
Engineer, the, 5, 11, 14, 18, 105
error by omission, 48
estimate, accuracy of, 65
estimation (of cost), 14, 33
evaluation (of tenders), 36
events, 75
experience, accumulation of, 7
exponential formula (for cost), 23
extension of time, 106
extrapolation (of value hour plots),
    95

Final Certificate, 106, 107
fixed price contract, 41
float, 78
FOB (free on board), 24
force majeure, 51
forecast (of completion), 92, 95, 105
form of agreement, 48
forward pass, 76
foundation, concrete, 21

general conditions of contract, 34, 41, 48
grapevine, 68
Green Book, The, 50
Guthrie modules, 25

historical data, 26, 55

inactivity, enforced, 51
indispensibly necessary work, 105
inflation, 56, 61, 96
initiation, 7
inspector, 92
insurance, 51
intermediate materials, 5
inverse cumulative probability, 68
invoices, 98
i/j diagram, 73

labour records, 92
Lang factors, 24
latest event time, 75
latest finish, 78
latest start, 78
law of the land, 51
laws of England, 50
let (of contract), 14
letter of invitation, 34
likely cost, 66
liquidated damages, 106
litigation, 43, 50
loan, 58, 60
logical dependency, 76
logical precedents, relationships, 74
lump sum contract, 41, 43, 90

Main Contractor, 3, 13
Maintenance Period, 106
management information systems, 91
man-hours, 92
mark-up, 14, 65, 66
material factor, 26
materials, 16, 17
mechanical engineering, 5

meeting of contractors, 10, 36
Miller factors, 24
mobilisation fee, 91
models (of bidding circumstances), 67

network analysis, diagram, 73
network in contract, 83
nodes, 73
normal distribution, 66, 70

objectives, 43
open tendering, 33
opportunity, recognition of, 7
Owner, 3, 12

payments, 58
penalty (to contractor), 45, 46
percentage complete, 92
peripheral equipment, 23, 25
PERT, 73, 84
phases (of project), 7
plans, drawings and diagrams, 35
plant, 17
precedence diagram, 73, 89
price, 9
price adjustments, 97, 98
price index, 96, 98
probability of winning, 66, 67, 69
product, 5
program of work, 50
progress, 56
project control estimate, 10
Project Engineer, 5, 16
Project Manager, 5

Quantity Surveyor, 13, 18, 20

raw materials, 4
receipts, 58
Red Book, The, 50
reliability, 8
resource allocation, 11
resource limiting, 81
resource smoothing, 80
resources, 7, 74, 78
responsibility, division of, 50
retentions, 50, 55, 58, 106
re-imbursible contract, 42
running costs, 9

sanction, 10, 13, 50
Schedule of Performance Tests, 106
Schedule of Take-Over Procedures, 106

scheduling, 11
scope, 16
sealed bid, 65
selection (of contractors), 35
site, 16
site agent, 16
site meeting, 51
special conditions of contract, 35
specifications, 8, 35
stanchions, 22
standard procedures, 12
statistical approach (to costing), 20
sub-activities, 92
sub-contractor, 4, 13
S-curve, 55, 91
S-curve, cumulative nature, 57

Take-Over Certificate, 106
target completion date, 45
target contract, 42
target cost contract, 44
technical feasibility, 7
tender, 14
tender documents, 10, 65
tender price, 65, 66

time cards, 92
time scale, 73
time value of money, 9
time, instant in, 75
time, elapsed, 75
turn-key project, 6

unit process, 20, 23
unit rate, 19, 21, 23
units of work, 19
unnecessary constraints, 81

value, 14
value hours, 92
variance, 90
variations, 41, 106
visible projects, 3

wall, double cavity, 21
wastage, 96, 98, 100
winning bids, 70
work types, 19, 20, 98
working conditions, 51
works, the, 17